THE SECRET ONLINE BUSINESS

HOW TO START & OPERATE AN OUTSOURCING COMPANY FROM HOME

CHRISTINE M. MYERS

© Copyright 2021 - All rights reserved.

It is not legal to reproduce, duplicate, or transmit any part of this document in either electronic means or in printed format. Recording of this publication is strictly prohibited, and any storage of this document is not allowed unless with written permission from the publisher except for the use of brief quotations in a book review.

Legal Notice:

This book is copyright protected. This book is only for personal use. You cannot amend, distribute, sell, use, quote or paraphrase any part, or the content within this book, without the consent of the author or publisher.

Disclaimer Notice:

Please note the information contained within this document is for educational purposes only. All effort has been executed to present accurate, up to date, and reliable, complete information. No warranties of any kind are declared or implied. Readers acknowledge that the author is not engaging in the rendering of legal, financial, medical or professional advice. The content within this book has been derived from various sources. Please consult a licensed professional before attempting any techniques outlined in this book.

By reading this document, the reader agrees that under no circumstances is the author responsible for any losses, direct or indirect, which are incurred as a result of the use of the information contained within this document, including, but not limited to, — errors, omissions, or inaccuracies.

Ordering Copies in Bulk:

DrumRoll Press products are available at special quantity discounts for bulk purchase through Amazon.com. Fund-raising, educational programs, and sales promotions are encouraged for outreach to disadvantaged and minority groups around the globe. For details, please write to: DrumRoll Press, 4771 Bayou Blvd. Suite 187 Pensacola, FL 32503 or contact email: drumrollpress2021@gmail.com

CONTENTS

Foreword   vii
Preface   ix

1. PLANNING YOUR FUTURE   1
   Personal Development   4
   Goal-Setting   5
   The Business Plan   12
   SBA Research   14
   The Last Word on Planning   15
   Summary   16

2. KEEP IT SIMPLE & PRODUCTIVE   17
   Economics 101   18
   Where It All Began   19
   High Yielding Profit Machine   21
   The Perfect Storm   24
   Your Key Focus   27
   Bridge Costs Are Low   28
   Summary   29

3. A FOUNDATION FOR SUCCESS   32
   Beyond Business Cornerstones   33
   Before You Open Your Doors   33
   Developing Your Website   37
   Tips for Building Your Site   38
   Online Presence   42
   Outside the Internet   45
   Labor Costs   49
   Value Yourself   50
   Summary   51

4. BLUEPRINTS FOR SUCCESS   52
   Finding a Rich Market   53
   Be Organized   59

A Day at the Shop	61
Emails and other Communications	62
Your Clients Determine Your Profits	64
Summary	65
5. TOOLS FOR YOUR SUCCESS	**66**
Time is $$$ Valuable	67
Financial Business Smarts	68
Our Business Secrets	70
Financial Rules to Live By	75
Credit Score and Ratings	76
Summary	81
6. SCORING OVER YOUR COMPETITION	**83**
Industry Competition	84
Impeccable Service = High Profits	84
Attend Networking Events	86
Expert Marketing Tips	86
Digital and Social Media Campaigns	87
Summary	95
7. NECESSITIES FOR GROWTH	**97**
Toss The Hats	98
Leadership	99
Plan and Execute	101
Summary	102
8. CONTRACTS	**103**
The Devil is in the Details	105
Thorough Inspections	109
Who is the Client?	111
Negotiate Until Satisfied	112
Deadlines and Completion Dates	114
Tips For Longevity	114
Summary	115
9. POLISHING YOUR PROCEDURES	**117**
Action Steps	118
Your Office	120
Procedures for Bidding Jobs	123
Working Up a Bid Manually	124

A Word on Merchant Accounts	126
Summary	127
Final Words	129
References And Suggested Reading	135

FOREWORD

~

In 2014, Christine joined in partnership with her husband, who owned and operated a custom awning manufacturing business for 12 years prior to uniting forces. Christine expanded their company using free organic marketing strategies propelling them to a new level of prosperity. Canvas Back Awnings LLC became a thriving awning & shade company serving the entire Southeastern Region of the U.S. and beyond. Together they hold patented products valuable to the future of the awning and shade industry.

Christine's entrepreneurial spirit succeeded her father's business acumen, who owned and operated a cash control systems business with under 20 employees for about 45 years. Christine began her entrepreneurial journey at 24 years old, opening a janitorial service company serving residential and commercial clients while attending college full-time pursuing her marketing degree. Reaching high-level retention of accounts within one year, Christine sold her profitable cleaning business and completed her degree in business marketing. After achieving her short-term personal goals in entrepreneurship and education, Christine worked as an independent contractor in the beauty industry for 25 years while pursuing various marketing ventures online and offline. Meanwhile, she accumulated knowledge and experience in several business areas including sales, management, digital marketing, contract negotiation, administration, and much more. Before her career in the beauty industry, Christine even traveled as a flight attendant internationally for a well-known airline now defunct.

Her hands-on experiences in business are fully expressed within this book as an honest and assertive personality. She spares no challenges faced as an entrepreneur, inspiring the reader to take action within their own set of circumstances, reasoning with a risk vs. reward approach to success that the reader can comfortably achieve with confidence and commitment.

Small business owners are the bedrock to our capitalist economic system, and is not a venture to be taken lightly. For those individuals ready, willing and brave enough to take the leap to becoming an entrepreneur, this book is for you.

The Secret Online Business: How to Start & Operate an Outsourcing Company from Home is an excellent example of building a business with integrity, vision, and best practice principles to ensure financial freedom for the entrepreneur. A highly recommended read.

PREFACE

"However difficult life may seem, there is always something you can do and succeed at." ~Stephen Hawking

---

Whether you are looking for a new business venture or have a clear idea of your company plans, the methods, tools, and strategies you'll learn within these pages will forge a clear path to success and wealth. Each business owners' desired future is unique and must be purposeful and committed. You need to know why this direction works for you and keep it in front of your goals. Without a "why," you won't stay motivated during the tough times.

Even if you feel you are in a dead-end job, unable to bring home the paycheck you believe you deserve or are tired of making someone else wealthy, working yourself into the ground is not a business owner's preferred method of making money, far from it. Working for yourself needs to be easy and efficient, and this book will guide you in avoiding costly mistakes and building a business that functions with efficient systems in place.

Most entrepreneurs desire the following:

- Decrease their working hours
- Increase their income
- Build an enjoyable, sustainable business
- Establish a sizable retirement account
- Spend more time with family
- Autonomy
- Add your main reason here:_____

Many affluent entrepreneurs assert, "Never let your business run you." Easier said than done! Working 14 hour days, seven days a week, will not only be non-productive, but it will turn a new entrepreneur into a burnt-out, short-tempered boss. Within the pages of this book are specific ways you can become efficient in all of your busyness so you can make time for the things you enjoy most, like spending time with family or relaxing on a beach on vacation.

In this book, you will find the gems of starting and running a profitable outsourcing or subcontracting business, but tedious processes found in many business books are not found here. *The Secret Online Business: How to Start & Operate an Outsourcing Company from Home* is full of incredible tips from the experts on how to avoid pitfalls many new business owners experience that can easily cost thousands of dollars in unnecessary expenditures resulting in wasteful spending, or even put them out of business in the first year! Within these pages, you will learn to:

- Learn Digital Marketing SEO tips from experts
- Define your Personal Blueprint for Success
- Reduce Ad Spend through Social Media Platforms
- Secret Tips to Increase your FICO Score
- Look like a Well-Established Business immediately
- Negotiate Contracts like a pro
- Additional Streams of Income ideas
- Learn valuable Personal Development Skills

And much more...

I will also share candid personal stories of surprising experiences I encountered as a small business owner and how I overcame many challenges faced by small business owners by always keeping my eye on the prize. I do include basic information and resources of the setup process, but not in minute detail because there are many resources available online and at the back of this book. However, you will gain valuable insight into the business world as if you were a seasoned entrepreneur before even beginning. Let me become your mentor for just a while.

My name is Christine Myers, and my husband and I have 20 years of business and industry knowledge to share, launching you to greatness in operating your own profitable company with low monthly expenses and stress.

Our journey to success came by way of the awning, canopy, and shade structure industry. This business can begin with a phone, printer, mailbox address, and a computer with internet, working from a couch or desk at home, needing very little start-up capital. Your "work from home" schedule governs your days and the best part of all...

Make More Money Than You Can Imagine!

I want to begin with a simple, effective, and high-yielding business structure which you can launch easily, achieve a lucrative business profit quickly, and bring yourself security and wealth for your near or far future. By already doing all the hard work, I'm giving you the golden nuggets of our success to apply to your own business, allowing you to not only make a high income but gain extensive insight.

Whatever industry you choose, these methods are the successful business strategies you've been searching for all along. When you apply these ingenious tips, you'll have all you need and explain in easy-to-understand and manageable steps.

Are you weary of office dramas, overbearing bosses, working hard for someone else, and hoping to get time off so you can watch your child's softball game? Becoming an entrepreneur is a serious commitment, but the benefits are incredible. It means taking vacation time on your terms, avoiding daily commutes, shopping when everyone else is working, being available for your family when they need you. But to have these visions materialize, you not only need your own business, but you also need it to be profitable. So look no further than this book because you've found the answers to end your financial hardships and career anxieties.

Let me introduce 'The Secret Online Business.'

What makes this online business so secret? It's the awning and shade industry or any outsourcing business! Few have found their riches, yet commercial real estate, restaurants, hotels, and apartment complexes place high demand for them. It's the business no one thinks of until it's necessary. But when the need does arise, finding an attractive, well constructed, custom-made awning can be frustrating, and for many, not to mention the unknown facts of installation needs and considering the structures will stand up to the test of time.

I want to share one of the stories that brought my husband and me to the bountiful life we live:

We became partners in Clearwater, Florida. There, the awning competition was fierce, even though our products outperformed many of our competitors. After losing contracts to awning companies that were seriously undercutting the market, we carefully and methodically considered expanding our company and corporate "office" to the Emerald Coast of Florida.

Our internet presence was off to a slow start in the first couple of months, but we expected it would take that long to get consistent calls; however, we were inundated with projects quickly! Pensacola and the surrounding areas were ripe for our quality products and outstanding customer service. We became a sought-after supplier almost overnight, able to pick and choose our jobs while focusing on the commercial sector (with a large percentage of higher-paying jobs and fewer hassles than residential clients). Demand was high, so we began selling surplus leads of residential projects and some smaller jobs to other companies and subcontracting out the larger, more profitable projects.

The only thing I ask of you is to sit back, absorb all the details and methods explained in this book, and apply what you learn to your awning or other industry strategies. But before we do that, I want to share our successful business secrets with those looking for a simple entrepreneur strategy that brings wealth while demanding minimal effort... eventually. Not only will you find wealth, but you'll gain a deep satisfaction and confidence, experienced only when you're in control of your income and your future. Don't expect overnight success or money for nothing. This type of methodology is not a get-rich-quick scheme, far from it. Real businesses take time to sprout and grow, with a commitment to longevity. It's really up to you how fast that will be.

By now, you may be wondering how much money you can make in profits running an awning or outsourcing company. While there are no guarantees in any business venture, you must weigh the risks and rewards. It is a very personal matter not to take lightly. Determine your success by the commitment you make to your business. The economic climate is an apparent uncontrollable factor, but you can control the outcome of your business by paying attention to the economic cycles in advance and hedging for protection against unexpected turns in the wrong direction. I have known of awning companies with hundreds of employees making over a million dollars a year in profits and others who shut their doors, putting hundreds of employees on the unemployment line. Who would have thought the world economic system would shut down due to a so-called "pandemic"? As I said, there is no guarantee. However, if you understand your clients' needs more than your competition and stay on top of your cash flow like a good business owner, you will succeed!

Note to the reader: I recommend websites and other resources in this book for your success, as I have used the same resources in my experience as an entrepreneur. I do not receive affiliate commissions from any of the sites or resources recommended to you.

Let's get started!

1

PLANNING YOUR FUTURE

"Some people dream of success, while other people get up every morning and make it happen."
~ Wayne Huizenga

Most likely, one of the reasons you picked up this book is because you are disillusioned with your present career, job, work, or business. In other words, the way you make money needs to change.

I FEEL your frustration and the feeling like you've hit a dead end. But I'm here to tell you that when you picked up this book, you already decided to say goodbye to the 9 to 5, mind-numbing J.O.B. (Just Over Broke). It's time to get rid of the anguish, stress, inadequacy, and unfulfilled dreams because now that you've begun reading this, you'll get inspired to begin strategizing your business plan, develop attainable goals, and take control of your life and your future wealth. Today you can become the entrepreneur you always dreamed of achieving.

However, before we go any further, being a business owner is extremely difficult by most standards: 4 of 5 businesses fail in the first five years; 4% reach $1,000,000 in revenue, and only 0.4% reach $10 million in sales. These are very long odds. (BOMBA 2021) Don't let this information discourage you or keep you working for someone else's dreams of success. Here is your chance to rise above the statistics and develop a foundation for success. Equip yourself with the ammunition provided in these chapters to corner your chosen market, and blow them away with your unparalleled products and services. The first requirement is that you must trust and believe in yourself.

The way to reach your goals is to:
research, research, research
learn a skill
gain confidence
take action

The above list is pretty self-explanatory, but you will find each of the four points mentioned in more detail in this book. The next subject is about gaining confidence, which is one of the four pillars to reach your goals.

> *"Success is no accident. It is hard work, perseverance, learning, studying, sacrifice, and most of all, love of what you are doing or learning to do."* ~ Pele

Before you begin your journey, you need to know the answer to this question:

What is an outsourcing company?

When you hire licensed contractors to manufacture products and installation services without hiring employees or doing skilled labor yourself, your only focus is the duties of an outsourcing company. The job of a subcontracting or outsourcing company is to draw the client to your business by employing marketing or advertising strategies and hiring the best independent contractors for any project. By keeping the project responsibility under your company name, the client and the contractor are relieved of specific responsibilities. Your expertise will be required as an outsourcing expert. Common industries well known for this type of business are interior designers and decorators or general contractors and distribution networks. However, if you choose the right industry, you won't need a "contractor" license to operate. Just by calling your company a "supplier" or "manufacturer," just a business license will suffice. The benefit for the client is the assurance that their needs will be met without the stress of handling several companies at the same time to complete a project. The benefit for you is the profits you make without the substantial overhead costs of running many types of businesses.

Twenty years ago, a business owner told me that his typical electric bill per month was $10k, so he had to sell a minimum of $20K in revenue per month just to break even in overhead expenses. This business was a glass-blowing art studio. How many people do you know who would buy a $20K piece of glass art? (the typical price of each piece) I would say this guy suffered from enormous stress to keep his business going month after month. The point I'm making with this example is that you want to have a business that makes you happy, one that is conducive to living in peace. You don't want to struggle with health issues because of stress or never get to see your family while they spend all your money without you.

Personal Development

Building positive habits in your personal and professional life is the key to a long, successful career as an entrepreneur. Establish daily routines prioritizing what you project for your future goes a long way in the grand scheme of things, not what feels good for today; that comes later and in small rewards. Whether you feel like it each day or not, take the necessary steps to make minor improvements. In chapter one of "Atomic Habits" by James Clear, he talks about the British team of cyclists who were mediocre at best for over a hundred years and never won the Tour de France during that time. With a change in coaches, they began to break records, win championships and become the top athletes of their sport. The new coaches implemented one small tweak at a time. By making one percent improvements in overlooked and unexpected areas, the team gained momentum in making significant performance improvements. We can apply this story to our own lives and businesses as an inspiration and encouragement.

SOME OF US may think we have to transform our entire lives all at once in the way we think and act to overcome hurdles that hold us back from becoming successful. But this task could be overwhelming for most, so they do nothing. Unfortunately, this mindset plagues most of the human population, and maybe it's the cause of many business venture failures, as I stated earlier. However, according to the experiments spelled out in "Atomic Habits," thinking this way is far from the truth. According to the previous story of the cyclists, all we need to do is make minor improvements to become successful. One downside to this concept might be that we want to rush the process, becoming impatient with ourselves. Evidence of this fact is found in the hundreds of books written about fad diets. The clock is ticking from one month to another when the bills are due, or the scale doesn't move, and our lives as humans get closer to inevitable death. The way to solve our negativity is to trust the process and give ourselves a chance to grow. All we have to do is change one small digestible decision at a time, and of course, read his book.

Goal-Setting

It may sound unusual to you, but before you develop your business goals, think of your personal and spiritual needs first, then your career goals last. Most new entrepreneurs have this concept reversed. With a lead in career ideals, the unwitting entrepreneur suffers a significant loss of personal satisfaction, and then later down the road, they realize that their personal and spiritual life suffered due to priorities in the wrong place. An example scenario would be, "I love to travel for business, but I also want to raise my children in a stable home when the time comes." You can't do business travel and raise children in a stable home at the same time. This scenario presents an apparent conflict of values from my point of view.

Knowing your values are so essential to defining what motivates you quantifiably. As I learned from Tony Robbins in his book, "Unlimited Power," first published in 1986, create a list of values first, narrowing them down to 10 in order. I highly recommend the book because it will change your life as it did for me a long time ago.

"If a person is getting one thing but vaguely wanting something else, he won't be happy or fulfilled. Or if a person achieves a goal but, to do so, violates his own belief about what is right or wrong, then turmoil results. To truly change, grow, and prosper, we need to become consciously aware of our own rules for ourselves and others and how we measure or judge success or failure. Otherwise, we can have everything and still feel like nothing. This is the power of the final and critical element called values." (Robbins, 1987)

. . .

I WILL GIVE you an example of a conflict of values that often happens to people and must be resolved by knowing the priority of your values list. "Freedom" has always been at the top of my list of values. I value my freedom in such a way as to supersede all other values, and the result of this value is that I will not work for anyone else, so I must work for myself due to this finding. Truthfully, I hate relying on anyone for my livelihood because my experiences in the workforce years ago were very traumatizing for anyone to go through. Chances are, you value freedom because you are reading this book to break free of working for someone else. Now here is my conflict: I also value "Security." To reconcile my "Freedom" and "Security" needs, I must know which is more important. "Freedom" is number one, then "security" is number ten on my list. Meaning, I would rather sacrifice my security to gain freedom if I need to choose only one scenario. What does this look like in real life? As I mature, my values regarding security are creeping up my list and becoming more critical than some of my other values. However, "freedom" still wins first place on my values list. However, now that I have far more experience in my life to provide the security, such as increased faith in my beliefs as a Christian, diversifying my wealth for retirement, and creating value in my gained skills and knowledge as a business owner. Therefore I can still maintain "freedom" and have more "security."

TAKE some time for yourself to visualize what you see your life looking like. Begin at the end and work backward to today. It's a fun and exciting time to slow your roll and think about your future rather than barreling through life without having a compass, as most people do. Personal development is crucial to begin your journey as an entrepreneur. Without knowing where you are going is like getting in your car and driving with no destination in mind. You will end up somewhere, but chances are it won't be a place you truly enjoy. Also, if you have no destination, someone else will be happy to create one for you, such as a family member who has their destination in mind.

BELOW IS a list of values and a worksheet for you to stop right now and figure this out. Don't go any further until you complete and satisfy the exercise!

I COPIED the list from https://jamesclear.com/core-values, which I believe to be a good starting point, but I suggest checking out the website for his free course on new habit-building skills as well. James Clear is the best-selling author of "Atomic Habits."

CORE VALUES LIST

- Authenticity
- Achievement
- Adventure
- Authority
- Autonomy
- Balance
- Beauty
- Boldness
- Compassion

- Challenge
- Citizenship
- Community
- Competency
- Contribution
- Creativity
- Curiosity
- Determination
- Fairness
- Faith
- Fame
- Freedom
- Friendships
- Fun
- Growth
- Happiness
- Honesty
- Humor
- Influence
- Inner Harmony
- Justice
- Kindness
- Knowledge
- Leadership
- Learning
- Love
- Loyalty
- Meaningful Work
- Openness
- Optimism
- Peace
- Pleasure
- Poise

- Popularity
- Recognition
- Religion
- Reputation
- Respect
- Responsibility
- Security
- Self-Respect
- Service
- Spirituality
- Stability Success
- Status
- Trustworthiness
- Wealth
- Wisdom

Your Top Ten **Values**

List your top ten values in order of importance below:

1. _____
2. _____
3. _____
4. _____
5. _____
6. _____
7. _____
8. _____
9. _____
10. _____

. . .

KEEP this list in your wallet, on your fridge, in your car, and your office. It will remind you of your priorities when you face tough decisions in the future. Develop time in your busy schedule to always give yourself a personal development checkup. For most people, values may change over time. And that's okay! Update and review your values regularly for accuracy. There are no wrong answers in this exercise. Experience is the key to longevity. This book covers the basic foundation of business knowledge you'll need, so keep learning and reaching for new ways to improve your business and personal growth. Spend at least 15 minutes of your day in motivational exercises such as YouTube videos or reading books to build your ego up. This part is golden, folks! The world will try to beat you down, so you must be the driver of your success!

ONCE YOU HAVE SPENT some time on your personal goals, you can devise a plan with specific milestones to reach your business goals. Create 6-month goals, 1-year goals, 3-year goals, and 5-year goals, even 10 or 20 years. If you want to build your business to increase revenue and client base for resale later or leave a legacy to your children, you should also structure that into your goal strategy.

KEEP YOUR PLAN SIMPLE; work on it as a monthly task on a specific day to make sure you are still on track and not off the rails of a crazy train. (Don't laugh, it can happen quickly!) You can always add or subtract goals as you progress because nothing is set in stone, and you are in the driver's seat. If you ever feel that you are losing control over your future, you can identify the wrong turns early and get back on track. It's better to catch it early and not five years down the road. Planning is Power! Sometimes the most challenging part of writing your plan is realizing it will come true for you. When you begin to understand the compartmentalization of time-slots, it will become easier to break them down to small bite-size, manageable chunks to digest. Visualizing your future should not be overwhelming to think about, nor should it scare you into a paralyzed state of being. It should feel empowering!

The Business Plan

Once you've established a clear vision for your future, you have narrowed down and weeded out what you will and will not do with your life. You should feel by now a burden lifted from your shoulders and liveliness in your steps. Joyfulness is what I call it. Now you are ready to begin your business plan. You may be wondering why you need one if you're not getting financial backing. The reason is simple: Every business venture needs a road map. It requires pinpointing if your milestones are reachable, recognizing small successes on the way, whereby arriving at your destination (pot of gold) at the end of the rainbow... within a set timeframe, of course!

BELOW IS a list of subjects to include in your business plan. Start with something simple and adaptable under each subject and repeatedly revise until you get it right. You will know when you're done because you will see a common theme throughout, and your confidence will grow because a magical thing happens: You will resolve the risk versus the rewards question. Every risk must come with a reward, and every risk can't be too risky. The reward has to be greater than the risk. Such is life!

- Executive Summary
- Company Objectives or Mission Statement
- Company Description
- Industry Analysis & Trends
- Target Market
- Competition
- Risk Assessment
- Sales Strategy
- Operations
- Software Applications
- Management Organization
- Sustainability Goals
- Financial Projections

ON EACH SUBJECT, you want to create a timeline of goals: Startup, six months, one year, two years, and so on, according to how you see the milestones reached. A popular book with everything you should know about writing a business plan is *Successful Business Plan: Secrets & Strategies* by Rhonda Abrams. Order the spiral book so you can use the worksheets in it. I highly recommend the book because it goes deep into the processes of your business plan. I have found nothing like it or even close to its depth and user-friendly readability.

. . .

You can start it, but you won't finish it before reading the last words of this book. A business plan can be simple and to the point, but you may need to complete a comprehensive, detailed report if you need funding or a business partner. Begin with simple milestones, then build on each. If you know of a successful business established and maintained in your industry of interest, see if you can find their mission statement online, dig into their website, and take many notes on their processes. Do this with a few companies you admire, both large and small, local and national.

Don't exclude other countries in your search. Figure out what they are doing right or wrong, and develop a method to scale their success to your business objectives. While researching, you will find the good, the bad, and the ugly in company policies and procedures or lack thereof. Pretend you are the customer searching for the right company. Learn from all three and create your objectives wisely based on these findings. In other words, don't just do what you think you can get away with. Your business plan can be simple, but make sure it is concise and complete. You'll want to establish what is important to you, what you must have, things you will not tolerate, and so on. Develop your list of 'must haves' based on your personal goals listed earlier as you outline your company.

SBA Research

An area that must not be overlooked is the resources available online published by the Small Business Administration. (SBA.gov) You will find a plethora of information on the website, leaving no stone unturned. Focusing on the minute details of starting a small business, you will have an additional resource to dig deeper into the logistics of a startup, operations, and financial calculations. I found the break-even analysis calculator to be especially helpful when I was preparing my business plan. Offline, there is a local chapter available in almost all populated cities around the U.S. Your tax dollars support it, so why not use it?

WHEN MY HUSBAND and I worked on our patent a few years ago, we received valuable advice from retired executives who volunteered to meet with us. The SBA is a valuable resource for the entrepreneur at any level.

The Last Word on Planning

You may need some backing if you plan to launch your business with increased capital. At the very least, you'll want a stable financial presence for your clients. Decide what kind of bank account you'll need and investigate the least expensive way to handle day-to-day transactions (keep this entirely separate from your personal accounts). Because the initial cost of beginning an outsourcing or awning business is low (you will require a 50% deposit to begin any project to cover expenses until the final payment, no exceptions), ensure you have a grasp of how your finances will progress throughout each project. The main concern is never to co-mingle funds between your business and personal accounts, making it very important to cover your personal expenses first. It requires discipline, which is why the goal-setting section is crucial to your success as an entrepreneur.

Summary

When planning your business future, begin with your personal values and purpose in life. Strategies listed in this chapter are the foundation on which to begin your journey as an entrepreneur. Without it, you will have no compass and no desirable future. If you don't plan it, someone else will, not in your favor but their own.

ONCE YOUR PERSONAL life goals are spelled out and reviewed, now you are ready to begin your business plan. Each topic is listed in the chapter for a simple plan focusing on most aspects of your chosen field of interest.

USE the free resources found in the sba.gov website for digging deep into your business plan and opening doors for support in funding, advice, and anything else you need. Your tax dollars fund the program, so why not try it?

THE NEXT CHAPTER will explain why a business in the awning and shade structure industry will give you almost guaranteed profits.

NOTES:

———————————————
———————————————

2

KEEP IT SIMPLE & PRODUCTIVE

"Success is where preparation and opportunity meet."~
Bobby Unser

Our knowledge and experience written in this book are the results of our 20 years in the awning and shade industry. It not only has all the information for setting up a successful small business in outsourcing, but includes extensive research and strategies my husband and I developed while building our successful and lucrative business in the awning and shade industry. I must say, however, our story isn't about sleepless nights and ramen dinners. We had a few rough spells here and there, which boiled down to recognizing the excess fat and streamlining our process. It's about finding the "sweet spot." (a golf term defining the perfect connection between the ball and your driver) For you, that means the perfect connection between the realm of possibilities and the life you envision for yourself and your family coming true for you. You have to envision it to attain it because no one ever stumbles upon success. It doesn't come knocking at your door either. You have to be ferociously hungry like a wolf who hasn't eaten for days. The top of the food chain is not for the minnows but the sharks. Are you hungry? How bad do you want it? Write it down in your new personal journal.

Economics 101

Market Explosion + Fizzled Supply = OPPORTUNITY for YOU!

FUNDAMENTAL ECONOMICS 101 begins with high demand for a product or service and low supply levels of that need. As long as supply levels are low, price levels remain high, and demand is met with a balance of the economic scales. Your job as an entrepreneur is to find the demand and create a business plan to supply it.

In our example as awning suppliers looking to expand our business, the Emerald Coast seemed like a great location where the looming threat of hurricanes is a yearly occurrence. All we had to do was research our business idea to confirm our suspicion that there might be a high demand for exterior shade structures in that region. Because we already knew that exterior shade and waterproofing structures are in high demand by commercial property owners around the country, yet are rarely satisfied with their choices in vendors for metropolitan areas, all we had to do when establishing a location was to evaluate three things:

1. If suppliers were offering quality awnings
2. If the market was in need of more suppliers
3. If our quality customer service was already present in the market

By answering these questions, we could determine if our business would prosper or struggle. Also, because the awning and shade structure business is reasonably specialized, we would drill down to see if our high quality and customer-oriented focus would outperform the competition. We knew we didn't want to work in a cutthroat market begging for business. There were many other places where we could be a big fish in a little pond if this didn't work out.

Where It All Began

My husband had been operating a successful awning business in Atlanta, Georgia before I met him. After being disillusioned with living in an overcrowded city, he moved to Clearwater, Florida, and set up his awning business there. He was a one-man show, operating all the jobs and debt-free. You can imagine how impressed I was with his business acumen, and it wasn't long before we merged my profitable business strategies with his successful, established operation.

When we began our partnership, we agreed to several 'musts' which our company committed to:

- Allow us a lifestyle to expand anywhere.
- Keep it small and customized.
- Always maintain integrity with clients.
- Manage a staff of just the two of us.
- Hire contractors to do the labor work.
- Sell in ten years for a profit.
- Retire in ten years

At the beginning of our fourth year, we held a patented product, had an efficient business system in place, and kept faithful to the promises we made to each other so far, including our focus on maintaining a small-sized operation.

Finding progressive ways to be efficient and profitable is vital when operating an awning company, or any other business for that matter. However, maintaining integrity in product and service standards while having a passion for helping people is a must in this business. Efficiency through progressive systems will give you the necessary advantage over your competition because you will be able to maintain low overhead and reinvest profits back into your business over time to hedge against economic and market fluctuations for generations to come. Though the strategies and business methods I'm going to teach you could work for any small business; I want to emphasize how profitable the awning business is. I'll often also use this as an example when discussing specific details and business structures to incorporate into your operation.

. . .

To reach the financial well-being goals we were aiming for, we kept to what we knew instinctively. Why reinvent the wheel? If you are already skilled in any other field, like financial services, mechanics, or another highly specialized skill, follow those same practices and ours for the consistent, over-the-top results you can achieve with your business. Our experience and knowledge will offer you an incredible edge when launching a new business, especially if you intend to keep your business small and manageable.

Whatever industry you are entering, please make a note to offer the best of whatever it is you're selling. Otherwise, these methods won't work. You won't have the dependable quality to fall back on if you have a complaint or need to relocate. Being the best you can be is the key to your highly successful business.

High Yielding Profit Machine

The awning industry offers business owners many positive attributes that other industries will never compete in. If scaled at your own pace of growth, you can start your business with very little capital and still expect to receive huge profits. Unless you happen to be well acquainted with the awning industry, getting into this line of business may never occur to you. Yet, when you realize the potential for orders and profits, you'll wonder why more people haven't stumbled across this gold mine before. Hence the title of this book: The Secret Online Business.

. . .

By offering a quality product in a low or non-competitive location, you can all but lock in the business of being the only professional awning company. And this business isn't like a barbershop or a grocery store. Chances are, you won't be having multiple repeat clients for a long time though they do happen. Your client is in it, most likely, for a one or two-time project, meaning that you will need to get new customers somehow. But the custom quality and exceptional attention to detail rank high in the word-of-mouth advertising category. When a client is happy with your work, they are more than excited to tell the world how excellent their supplier is:

- Easy to work with.
- Completed the work on time.
- Offered quality products and service.
- Staff kept them updated during project.

As I've mentioned, our business model could fit easily into many other industries. We chose the awning business because of our experience and knowledge in that industry. But this business model could work in many skill-driven industries even with saturated markets if you are willing to pay close attention to getting your name out there on the top of the Google search engine. Some examples include:

- pool builders
- boat covers
- landscaping or tree service companies

- specialized cleanup services
- sign companies
- specialized construction services
- handyman services
- custom window treatments
- interior designers & decorators
- and a host of other industries

I KNOW what you're thinking: "I don't know how to do any of those skills, and I don't want to carry a contractor's license for anything." Well, I have good news for you. You don't need to know any of these skills or carry a contractor's license. Does a barbershop owner need to go to school and receive a license to become a barber? The answer is no. I will show you throughout this book how you can subcontract or even sell leads without ever lifting a finger in labor work, and you shouldn't if you own the business. Your only job is to attract the client to you and match them with the contractor (who already has the license) who fits their needs. It's all about marketing, sales, and commitment.

THIS BOOK WILL INSPIRE you to think about the possibilities and research your chosen market, or you can even expand further and choose more than one. For example, a client may want a swimming pool for the family, but will also need a patio cover and porch with concrete pavers to add ambiance to the backyard. Wouldn't it be great if you as a liaison for the client, bring together all of those contractors under your company name and receive an income for your service, and a percentage as your profit? All you have to do is be the mover and the shaker for your clients, and they will be thrilled to pay you for your exceptional service and quality products. She won't need to know that you contracted out all the work. Neither will she know what companies you chose for her project. All she cares about is that she is satisfied with your work, and she can't wait to share the photos on Facebook with all of her friends. She trusts you to get the work done correctly, and that's all that matters to her.

The Perfect Storm

Let me show you a few reasons why this is the perfect storm for a new entrepreneur starting a business at this time in history:

MANY U.S. BUSINESSES are currently experiencing a paradigm shift, especially the awning industry. Younger generations, particularly children of parents who have operated a business for many years, are not continuing the family business when their parents retire. This shift in human history leaves many businesses wide open for grabs to the hungry entrepreneur, and the awning business is one of them.

MEANWHILE, over the last 30 years, corporations squeezed many small businesses out of their markets by severely undercutting prices (illegal and unethical). Then over time, without strong competitors in the way and a huge voice in government lobbying for their industries, profits replaced people in the workplace. One by one, customer service took the back seat in running a business. (Think of all the phone prompts, long wait times, foreign-accented answering services, complicated chain of departments handling your projects, hidden fees, deceptive marketing, and finally low-quality products) all of which adds up to bad business practices in our opinion! Many big corporations have lost their personal touch with the client because they already got too big and will never shrink back.

I'M WRITING this book one year after the worldwide Pandemic of Covid-19, and certain factors have changed history forever, such as low or no-contact business to business dealings, so you should expect never to have to shake hands or even meet with a potential client or supplier if you choose the direction of commercial property projects. Technology replaces the need for face-to-face contact by the use of online meeting rooms and other communication devices. Many industries are forced to comply with certain regulations that the awning industry is exempt from because the awning vendor never has to walk inside a building for any reason. In fact, it's always been our rule to never enter a building while on a property to install an awning.

ANOTHER RESULT of the worldwide pandemic is the influx of independent contractors into various markets because of lay-offs from work in 2020. Many of them are new entrepreneurs with minimal marketing experience but excellent skills. So they might be excited to get business from you as an outsourcing company. If you keep them busy, they won't have to pay someone to advertise for them. It's a win, win situation for everyone.

. . .

Can you see how this opportunity can work for you?

Our experience of failures and successes over the years can show you how your business can rank high very quickly on the Google search engine costing you $0 advertising dollars out of pocket, keep your overhead low, and manage your tight ship with minimal effort so you can enjoy watching all the profits fly straight to your bank account.

Researching the needs of the market you are interested in will give you the edge over the competition, and the markets which reach beyond technology and modernization will be the industries to move into. The awning and shade structure industry is leading the charge on creating those trade opportunities.

Because our company has always stayed on top of cash flow and looking for efficient ways to operate without sacrificing quality for our clients, we needed to make some changes on a core level of our business several years ago. We discovered an answer to our need for transportable frames without the high cost of shipping and spent the better part of three years tirelessly producing "The Smart Awning System." As of this writing, this patented product is not yet available to the public or private sector but will be very soon. It is truly ahead of its time in development and uses; however its owners are planning a campaign to license or sell the patent rights rather than mass produce it ourselves. We as business owners prefer to keep things simple and be patient in finding the right company to take on the product, rather than opening a facility and manufacturing the product ourselves. That is what this entire book is about; keeping it simple. We have to live the advice we give.

Your Key Focus

Here's a short description of how a 'middle man' works within an industry. Your business will connect the needy client to the producing supplier, and you maintain the flow of communication, customer service, and financial liquidity moving from order to completion. Exceptional service is the key to making this network relationship prosperous. You are the face of the purchaser and the manufacturer. You oversee the specifics for the customer's order and hire the manufacturer for the project, seeing the job through to the end. You will save your customer and the supplier from stress, mistakes, poor quality, and delayed completion. The term 'ringleader' comes to mind when describing your key focus. You become the person with a skillset for compassion, negotiation, and answers to their questions in a way they understand by keeping everything running smoothly like a well-oiled machine. Most issues transpire when there is a communication breakdown between the customer and the vendor.

COMPLICATIONS WILL OCCASIONALLY OCCUR with any business, but if we use the "Golden Rule" in our dealings with clients and suppliers, "treat others the way you would want to be treated," your company will lead the pack in your chosen market. Many companies have forgotten this foundational rule by cutting costs to make huge profits, meanwhile leaving the client frustrated and wondering if their product came directly from China! Rest assured, in this book, we'll discuss the solutions to almost any problem by avoiding negative situations in the first place, and usually, the answers are found within your iron-clad contracts.

Bridge Costs Are Low

From the client to the manufacturer, one could look at your business 'role' as a bridge. Acting as this "bridge" you'll soon agree, the many ways of serving both sides span multiple opportunities in many industries. Often, these roles are labeled as a distributor, a middle-man, or a network connector. Networkers are incredibly popular of late, and with the help of the internet, a computer, and a phone line, you can quickly put yourself in the driver's seat for business and revenue. Let's break down the necessary items you'll want to start with:

- Computer and printer
- Internet connection
- Phone
- Courier mailbox for your paychecks
- Business bank account to deposit checks

I WANT to make sure you understand how easy this will be. Your business thrives on conversations and relationships just as much as it does on measurements and orders. In the awning business, once you get your office set up:

- Retain reliable and experienced sewing contractors (they can work from anywhere)
- Contract a welding fabricator
- Once in a while you may need a graphics designer
- Retain a local contractor who can install awnings (a licensed sign company with all equipment, hourly workers, and insurance).
- Have a few fabric and notions suppliers with a fast delivery system in place

Your business will be operating by taking orders, contacting suppliers, and scheduling installations. It is that easy!

We will go into details on each of these points later in this book.

Summary

If you are in one of few critical industry operations, this will guarantee clients. The awning industry is one of them, but later in this book, we will offer some other suggestions to inspire you as well.

Finding the right business opportunity is crucial to success. You can be a great company offering top-notch service, but if you're in high competition for clients, high overhead expenses, or there's not a market for your product, the chances of success diminish. Start strong on an up-trending scale to the top, not the last in line to the bottom.

Some similar business models you may be familiar with include Realtors, Interior Decorators or Designers, and General Contractors. However, these types of professionals must carry a contractor's license to operate their business. Some don't, and that is the area of focus here.

The awning business is a lucrative industry among subcontracting companies that would easily qualify for a low-cost startup and minimal necessary systems in place.

It's easier to maintain a small-scale operation, especially at the start of your business. Suppose you have a lot of startup capital (which most of us don't), fight the urge to go big, or overspend. Focus on offering a quality product and service for each client, and your chances of success multiply.

The most important thing to remember is to place yourself in an optimal position by offering excellent service, having little competition, and keeping focused on your goals.

Your key focus is to be the "distribution network" of the business serving your client by becoming the "ringleader" who brings it all together.

. . .

IN THE NEXT CHAPTER, you will learn how to set up your business structure, website, delivery services, and email connections.

NOTES:

_____
_____
_____
_____
_____
_____
_____
_____
_____
_____

3
A FOUNDATION FOR SUCCESS

"Success is the result of perfection, hard work, learning from failure, loyalty, and persistence."
~ *Colin Powell*

Eventually, as your business becomes established in your chosen industry, you will be able to focus on growth and new revenue streams instead of playing the catch-up game of tending to irrelevant issues better handled by your team of competent employees or independent contractors. An excellent long-term business plan must be at the forefront of your beginnings, so you can be on the lookout for the opportunities that will propel you to the end goal: Financial Freedom!

Beyond Business Cornerstones

Begin small while you learn the industry you have chosen, and for most of us, that means starting with a home office. This can be done simply enough with an internet connection, phone, computer, shipping account, and a UPS mailbox. (Rather than a P.O. Box address, UPS offer addresses that look physical even though they are not.)

IF YOU START small in your home office, separating your personal and business life is essential to building your empire. If at all possible, make sure your 'office' is away from household routines and distractions. Keep your business defined while maintaining its integrity as a 'business.' But if you absolutely cannot fulfill this advice, don't let it delay you from starting your business.

Before You Open Your Doors

Before beginning any business venture, you must do your research, as we discussed earlier. Don't skimp on this time-consuming task. "Fools rush in," they say, and I believe this venture is no different. There are several things you will want to do before you launch your intentions to your potential customers. They are:

RETAIN FINANCIAL ASSISTANCE: Even if you don't hire an accountant to do your 'books' immediately, make sure you know how to handle business accounting, tax regulations, statements for licenses, and any other financial documentation you may need for your region. It would be wise to hire a

CPA to start your books and perhaps do your quarterly reports and taxes. Handling the day-to-day transactions you may feel the need to do yourself in the beginning to save money. We recommend a software system to store receipts and reconcile all transactions for tax purposes. You can also download the app right to your cell phone for easy access and take snap-shots of receipts. Most CPA's can recommend the software they typically use. Recently I found a company that is amazing for small businesses called 1800accountant.com . I would recommend them for tax planning advice and service that will save you thousands of tax dollars every year.

DETERMINE YOUR BUSINESS STRUCTURE: When I'm discussing structure, I am focused on how you are setting up your business: Sole Proprietorship or Partnership is not recommended for any subcontracting business because your personal assets can become vulnerable to lawsuits, and there are now strict limitations on obtaining business insurance with either structure.

A LIMITED LIABILITY COMPANY (LLC), S or C Corporation would qualify for carrying an insurance policy. Carefully consider how you want your business to operate. I'm not going to go into each option, only to state that you want to make sure your business is separate from your assets as a preventative measure if unforeseen circumstances occur in your personal or business life. Structuring under an LLC will easily allow you to simplify your financial reports and tax requirements while also fulfilling requirements for business liability insurance. While you can file an LLC yourself,

I do not recommend this method as a wise choice unless you are familiar with business structures. There are companies and attorneys online that will do everything for you at a meager cost compared to the do-it-yourself filing. Remember, time is money, and leaving it up to the professionals frees up your time to grow your business to pay for such professional skills.

RETAIN LEGAL ADVICE: Due to the obscure legalities of running a business, its sound advice to have legal representation when assembling your company and retainer for ongoing consultation. Your contracts will be rock solid, and your clients will respect your company. If you are on a stringent budget initially, I recommend searching online for copyright-free generic templates of contracts and forms, then tailor each by adding your business information and specifics.

GET BUSINESS INSURANCE: Having business insurance is imperative when owning a subcontracting company, not just to hedge your business against unforeseen circumstances like illness or property damage, but also a liability policy for your clients. When serving the commercial sector of an awning company, most corporations require us to carry a liability policy of one million dollars minimum. (don't worry, the premiums are low cost to you) On rare occasions the client will ask for an increase of your policy to two million dollars, or a "rider" on the policy stating some other addition to the policy like a "bond" or "Worker's Comp." For our company, worker's compensation was never an issue. We obtained a "worker's comp exempt" form from the state because we only had two employees, my husband and me. At this writing by law in Florida, you can file "exempt" if less than four employees work for the company.

BEFORE CONTRACTS ARE EVER SIGNED, you can always make changes with your agent when necessary, but one million is the minimum you should always carry. The business client will require a Certificate of Insurance form before the commencement of a project to protect against damage to their property, even though you will be sub-contracting the work. Acquire your policy from a reputable company with a fast turnaround to provide your client with a COI. You will need all pertinent information from the client on the name and address of the company in charge of paying for the project called "Insured listed". The client who signs your invoice may not know they need this information, so it could take a day or two for them to get it to you before you forward the information to your agent.

YOU SHOULD ALREADY HAVE your sub-contractors lined up and ready to begin the project. The obvious contracting to hire out is the specialized skills you don't have, such as the welder, sewer, graphics designer, and installers. Your valuable time as the brains of the operation should be focused on creating wealth and value for your company, not answering phones! Still, when you can afford it, the sooner you retain reliable help to answer phone calls, enter invoices, handle website management, and do the ordering/shipping, the sooner you will be able to develop the growth of your business by creating new avenues for revenue, or widening your scope of services.

Developing Your Website

Contract a reputable and capable site host (company). We designed it ourselves because we wanted complete control over our site, and GoDaddy was perfect for our needs as an awning company. Because my husband and I did not want to learn web development or dabble in web-building technology, we searched for user-friendly drag and drop design software, which was an excellent answer for getting our website's online presence on Google's search engine. GoDaddy offers tutorials for the beginner, but it was so easy that I never needed the tutorials. GoDaddy has unbeatable 24/7 customer service for late-night designing questions if you get stuck. I was very nervous about taking on this project, but it took us a week to create our website, and looking back, I have no regrets. If you don't want to create the website yourself, it can be a considerable expense hiring most companies. If you want to have your host write content and design the pages, make sure you are using an established company that can accomplish this and trains you on maneuvering within your site to upload photos regularly or a good contact you can send photos to them quickly. It isn't a big deal until you want to add to your content or photos.

I DECIDED to create my site because we had a bad experience before that time, paying obscene amounts of money for a company to create and host our site. It didn't drive traffic to it, and then the company went out of business a year or two later, leaving us with a site we couldn't get into and update. It was a big waste of our dollars because we were uneducated about such matters at the time. Fortunately, we are unstoppable in solving problems and getting on to the next venture.

Tips for Building Your Site

If you are creating your own pages and content, I'm proud of your initiative. It can be a simple process for a service-based industry, though if you decide to work nationally or globally, you'll want further knowledge for the best results with search engine ranking.

Keywords and phrases **for your site:** Find as many related words to your industry as possible. A simple search on WordStream Keyword Tool will give you many 'keywords,' and the free trial extends for seven days. Use as many of these words, naturally, within your website pages. Don't overload or use these words without a composed flow. Search engines are brilliant in finding "keyword stuffing" and will lower your rankings if they sense any deviation from an attractive and informative page. Use the words wisely, and your site will yield significant organic traffic. Use keywords in your domain and company name if possible, such as the word "awning". Using key search terms automatically ranks you high, as you are providing logical and relevant information quickly.

Name **your photos wisely before uploading:** Before your company completes a project of its own to display on your site, you will need to borrow or purchase someone else's photos to legitimize your company. We never had to do this as a business, but keeping your needs in mind as my priority in writing this book, I suggest asking your sewing sub-contractor to allow you to use their work or copyright-free awning photos from a company such as Shutterstock or Pixabay. Eventually, your company will acquire photos from its jobs, so keep that in mind as you name them. You can use my method to increase your SEO ranking by using keywords in the name of the image. For example: 'orange+entrance+awning' Now you're in the big leagues! Your photo and website can now show up on a search for "images" when someone searches for an orange entrance awning on Google. Before we go any further on uploading photos of projects, I want to make it crystal clear that the photos must be of good quality and have a "watermark" on every one of them (keeps internet trolls from stealing your work). It takes time to do this, but you must create two copies, one with and one without a watermark.

FOR YOUR FILES, use a retrieval method of photos. Think about the easiest way to retrieve your photos and images before picking a system to name and store them. If you file by structure, use the same word in the title description. If you want to file your images by date, list them first before the description or job. Remember that you'll eventually have hundreds of photos and will often be searching intently for a specific one. By naming them so you can retrieve them quickly, you will be saving yourself hours of search time trying to find an image you remember. Here's an example of my filing system: An invoice number which already has a date listed, and the last number is 4, which is the fourth original quote I sent that day: 1123214 then add the color and style: O- orange and E- entrance = 1123214OE,

Choose the right system that works for you and keep a record of code terms.

Add links to other sites: By adding links, you are 'enriching' your viewers' experience, scoring higher in the algorithms of the Google search engine. Ensure the site is relevant to your content and ask the website owner if you can link to their site. They will often be overjoyed to have you market their site and might also link their relevant content back to you if appropriate. Inserting a link into most pages is easy; just go to their website and "copy" the URL and "paste" it into your website images. Look for the 'Tools' tab, or ask 'Help' to add a link to your page for further assistance. Below are some ideas for accomplishing the task:

Add **vendor logos to your site:** It not only gives you credibility and gives a respectable 'nod' to your vendors, but Google algorithms love the energy. First, download your vendors' logo from their site or search Google "images," upload it to your site, and paste their URL link on the logo image link window. Now your potential clients can view your vendors' websites from your site to see the products your company offers. On our site, we added an entire page dedicated to our vendors' logos and added the URL to the logo photo so when the potential client goes to our site and hovers over the logo and clicks it, a new window opens with our vendor's website. As your company grows, you can also add logos of corporate clients your company has serviced. Adding links to your website portrays your company as having 'expert status.' Think of every link you add to your site as powering more electricity to it. The more 'electrified' your site, the higher the rank on Google searches.

Use 'hovering' **over your images:** The newer, more modern websites have a feature that Google ranks higher than others for a more user-friendly experience. Have you ever been online searching for a company, and find the website to be so outdated that you just sigh and move on to the next one? I'm sure you have! Google wants the internet surfer to enjoy their surfing experience, so the modern website will always rank higher as long as the keyword is relevant. "Hovering" is one of those features that algorithms recognize as "modern". You can link your images and content to other interesting information, such as when you write content about retractable awnings, post a video of a retractable awning in action.

Use links **in your emails and newsletters:** This is an easy way to get your email list to see your website or other pertinent information about your company. Another addition to this method of visibility, you can join an email campaign. Some are free to join, others charge a monthly rate, but if you choose to go this route to build a list, you might as well choose a company that contains links to Google reviews directly to your company search results, such as Constant-Contact. Your happy client can conveniently leave a 5-star review directly from your closeout email, which otherwise you may not ever receive.

. . .

ADD MOVEMENT TO YOUR PAGES: Search engines rank 'movement' high on their algorithms also. Photo slides of your finished projects on your home page will WOW your potential clients into hiring you for their next project.

Online Presence

You'll also want a website which will show your potential and current clients what you offer, how your product can help them, and your business mission (why you are in business and how you view your place in your community), any upcoming news or new products, and how they can contact you. Adding specialty pages, such as lead magnets that often promote a special offer or a timely blog if you feel you are attracting clients interested in the product (such as high-end contractors or national accounts), can also pull in more interest, more business. When creating your site, you need to be aware of your clients' needs and desires. Keep in mind whom you're client represents. If you are serving the commercial sector, your target market is the business owner or the corporation. But the final decision maker is the owner of that shopping center who hired the property manager. All of their management team must be in agreement with the owners. As Kevin McArdle, my mentor in sales training and best practices taught, 'What's in it for me?' the client might say." Make your content stand out from the rest by showing the client that your company can go above and beyond the rest of the competition by offering to solve the problem they are facing.

BELOW ARE a few terms you should know to get the right team working for you or creating your own website:

. . .

SEO (SEARCH ENGINE OPTIMIZATION): Formulating attractive keywords on a website page coincides with a person's words when searching for a given item or topic. This is also known as on-page SEO. There is also off-page SEO (rates how links on your page relate to other web pages), technical SEO (uses page design and usability as a ranking factor), local SEO (ranks locations close to the address originating the search), app store optimization (large retail apps such as Apple Store and Google's Play Store are configured in the algorithms), and YouTube SEO (similar to app store optimization, utilizing one of the world's most popular search engines. Ranking high on YouTube SEO is pure gold) Keyword and key phrase are the 'keys' a search engine (such as Google or Bing) uses to show the best results for a web inquiry (or search). The search engine uses algorithms (complex sorting techniques) to give an inquiry the best results. These are the words you use within your trade and someone would use to look for your services. For instance, a bakery would use bread, and an awning company would use, well, awning! Search engines drive traffic to your website when you use relevant keywords to describe your site.

DIRECT TRAFFIC: These are people who go to your site directly, entering your website address themselves. They already know of your company, either by a business card, word of mouth, brochures, ad campaigns, or your suggestion. In other words, they would have no other way of contacting your site other than knowing of you. Marketing often generates direct traffic through links and website addresses.

. . .

Referral Traffic: Your clients will find your website throughout the web through 'referral traffic,' either by affiliate reference, an article that lists your business in its content, or someone who chooses to follow a link in another site. If you focus on sharing your website in many different places to attract referral traffic, be aware that you risk being tagged by algorithm search bots. You will get penalized, which will compromise your organic traffic. Just make sure you use high-quality links without any spamming. If you use this technique naturally and wisely, you'll be good to go.

Organic traffic: When you are visited by 'organic traffic,' it is because your website was found through an online search, using either Google, Bing, Yahoo, or other search engines. These are the people who come to your website page (s) using keywords or phrases to find you. When you increase your SEO retention, this traffic will increase your ranking on the search pages and analytical numbers. A big secret to keeping your ranking high is to keep your content of good quality. Use direct and referral traffic tactics wisely, and your content naturally gets ranked higher, increasing the organic traffic.

Social Traffic: People will come to your website from social pages, such as LinkedIn, Facebook, Instagram, and Pinterest, looking for your images to give them ideas for dressing up their home or business. Post quality content often on these social sites and keep it separate from your personal life. If you have a blog on your site, tag it in every post, and vice versa. Keep the 'flow' between all the sources current, so the content keeps refreshing and the search engines 'love' your website! Views of your site will increase dramatically over a short period of time, guaranteed!

OUR STRATEGY for free advertising happened by a "happy accident," as Bob Ross, the artist, would always say. After we listed our company with "Google Business" in our main geographical areas throughout Florida, they sent reports to our email address listed. We could open the email they sent and post awning project photos we procured. This process took literally 2 minutes to accomplish. Calls for awnings came in like crazy right after a post. Make it a point to post as many photos and content as possible in a consistent way, and guess what? It's All Free!

Outside the Internet

Phones, Communication, and Answering Services: Your phone is your connection to gaining customers and placing orders. Aim always to have a live person answering incoming calls. Use a professional greeting, smile when you speak, and make sure you are thorough in your answers without being lengthy and redundant. Be patient without being condescending, and share your passion for your industry with enthusiasm and quality assurance.

WHEN YOU'RE JUST GETTING STARTED, you'll probably be answering all the calls yourself, but eventually, you should choose to hire a quality answering service that keeps your business personal and welcoming. Hire an agency (some bill their fees on a per-call basis) or person (family members love to help here) to answer your incoming calls. Forward current clients to your cell phone for their questions and concerns which would deserve immediate attention, and take messages from your answering service for people who are interested in quotes or more information. In other words, separate customers' calls to your cell whom you've already bid on, who is negotiating an order, from new calls coming in re-routed to your call center. You may also want to consider using your landline to place outgoing calls to potential clients. You'll lessen dropped calls and increase the reliability of keeping the call connected. Using the call-forwarding option will further answering your clients' needs if you leave the office.

THE BOTTOM LINE IS THIS: Station your landline as the receiving phone number for all calls. Add a short prompt system to divert new numbers to a call center or sales representative for general information and new bids. Current clients' projects should directly forward to your cell or their salesperson, which will be another prompt when they call. All phone numbers will be recorded so you never miss out on a potential project.

PURCHASE A UPS MAILBOX: When you begin shipping and receiving items, you'll realize that having the service of a trusted mail courier is imperative. Purchase your 'home base' mailbox address in the largest city you'll be servicing, and add the address to your website and on all of your communications: Invoices, contracts, bids, and business cards. Even digital advertising should include this information so that you can receive payments and items without delay. Also, your vendors will be shipping supplies to a reliable location during business hours while you may be on the road somewhere else and not your office. NEVER use your home address as your business address!

CREATE AN EASILY ACCESSIBLE DATABASE: Quotes, contracts, and contact information should be organized as a system for immediate accessibility, even the contacts who don't order. Inevitably, when I believe a person isn't going to hire us, they call back two weeks later and want to schedule an order. To look professional and save yourself time and money in addition to building your reputation, have all information at your fingertips.

KEEP ALL QUOTES: In the early years, when the slow season came around, we would pull out our old quotes and call all our contacts. Some never chose a company to replace their awnings, or the employee handling the project would leave the company and drop the ball on getting their awnings. Just let them know you follow up with old bids and want to be sure they are satisfied before permanently closing their file. If they show interest, I recommend telling the potential client you can re-bid at a discount price if they buy now. Make sure that you have the wiggle room to negotiate a lower price before making the promise, and in return, they only get a short period to make a decision. We have always been able to pick up a job or two by using this method. If the client has been satisfied through another company or changed their mind, now you can toss out their contact information with confidence that you have done everything possible. Follow up with bids and keeping the contact as long as the customer is still looking will always be a go-to task when you need the extra money.

I ALWAYS KEEP a hard copy of all records. I've known too many business owners whose computer systems have 'crashed' and left them with nothing but a frozen hard drive. If you aren't the type to keep paper copies, back up your system (at the end of each day) with a reputable storage company, or copy to flash drives. Some are heavily encrypted for high security, while others tend to be another system to safeguard your information. Whichever you choose, have a backup source of some kind for your company.

MORE OFTEN THAN NOT, in B2B sales, the turnover of employees, or a new property management company, a sale or restructuring of a company, your company name will inevitably be forgotten when it comes time to replace that awning down the road. It's best to keep a list of contracts completed for at least the life of the awning, so when it's time to replace it, you will have all the details to contact the client again. They will look up at your awning and wonder who made it. We solved the problem of forgetfulness with our Q.R. code sticker or label either directly on the awning itself or the window facing. Our invention, a freebie for the awning industry back in 2008, the "all" label identifies all the information about the awning so the potential return client can see on their cell phone everything related to the project down to the color number of the fabric. Quotes and styles change, but if you have a reference point from which to work, you can quickly revise measurements or materials needed at your fingertips. If your website allows free unlimited pages, your Q.R. code can go directly to the page you created for the client, and you can "hide" the page from the general public.

Keep a Record of Passwords: Have an updated running log of your passwords in a hard copy form or flash drive. If something happens to you or your family, the business will continue to move forward without hesitation until you return.

Labor Costs

As you build your company, labor costs can make or break a bid. We always hired specialized contractors for work because they take full responsibility for craftsmanship, carry insurance, and set prices beforehand. You may notice their pricing is higher than an hourly employee completing a project, but that's the tradeoff. Deciding which choice is best for your company is only something you can determine. Knowing the labor cost before the job starts gives everyone a fair expectation of the tasks at hand and the cost of its completion. My advice is that while you are new in the business and still learning yourself, hire out the work to contractors, then add to the payroll one employee at a time if you choose this route. Never pass up an excellent opportunity for a loyal and worthy employee opportunity. Good help is hard to find, so don't rush to hire someone without a full-scale background check and application review.

. . .

If you hire more than two employees who work full time, you not only commit to allotted hours, but you have to pay worker's compensation to the state as a rider on your business insurance. Using interns from universities or temporary service companies can bypass this deficiency while also screening workers for a potential full-time position when needed. Don't sacrifice your business reputation and profits with a less than adequate employee. Keeping a close watch on your business' capital and cash flow is never time wasted.

As I said earlier, we chose not to hire employees in our business. All of the work we did not want to do was contracted out to professionals while we focused on staying true to our personal needs. This business concept should not be frowned upon as a business owner because just like relationships in the real world, it's easier to get into, but difficult to get out of. *Caution* and *Prudence* are words that come to mind when I think of hiring employees.

Value Yourself

Always pay yourself first. You can do this as a regular payroll check or automatic transfer, but always do it. If you're working with very low capital initially, make sure you cover at least your personal expenses. If you find it difficult to pay yourself to cover personal expenses, I highly recommend finding ways to lower those expenses.

Most savvy entrepreneurs delay self-gratification for awhile until their business is more established and profitable. Don't be one of those people who gets a $20K final check for a project and blows it on frivolous consumer goods, leaving nothing for the lean seasons. Be the person who is responsible with money by making rules for yourself to follow and stick to them. Then you can give yourself a bonus when the projects are completed.

Summary

Having an excellent reputation is more than just having satisfied customers. It brings more business by word of mouth (free advertisement) and exceeds industry standards. Taking care of your clients will never be a wasted effort.

HIRE out the tasks you can't do, and eventually tasks you can do but don't want to do, allowing time for you to build your business and achieve your goals.

DETAILS OF STRATEGIES and methods outlined in this chapter can streamline your process.

IN THE NEXT CHAPTER, you will learn the strategies and goals that were successful for our business and how marketing and organization will streamline your business operations.

4

BLUEPRINTS FOR SUCCESS

"The secret of your success is determined by your daily agenda."
   ~John C. Maxwell

I've touched on this briefly in previous chapters, but here we're going to begin digging into the details of creating a successful business. Remember the 4 points I mentioned in chapter one to achieve a goal ? Now I will cover the 'research', 'learn a skill', and 'take action' points in detail as we move through this chapter and beyond.

WHAT DOES a consumer think about when purchasing goods or services?

- high-quality
- availability
- fair price

- customer service

SOMETIMES A CONSUMER WILL COMPROMISE something for a great price; we call it "getting the biggest bang for your buck," but generally, these four attributes govern most purchases. Your company can fulfill all of them without compromising adequate profit. You will have cornered the market with your products and services, and clients will share a review online or tell their friends about your company. And that, my friend is priceless!

Finding a Rich Market

What do you suppose happens when a company or business has all of these things in place and yet, can't seem to accumulate revenue and make a profit? Most likely, it has to do with these four outside factors:

- economic uncertainty
- lack of industry necessity
- low market demand
- high competition (high supply)

IT'S hard to stop the bleeding while it's happening, but you may be able to prepare for any situations that could occur. The smartest thing you can do for your business is to hedge a wall of protection around these factors as the big business boys do.

. . .

Economic Uncertainty: As we had already seen in 2020, economic uncertainty can happen without warning. Or was there a warning? The answer is yes! Before the Covid-19 pandemic reached the U.S., it began in China. Before it was in China, a patent was filed and approved by the USPTO in 2012 listed under The Pirbright Institute (U.K.), the C.D.C. (U.S.), and Rockefeller. (I reviewed the patent myself before it was removed from the internet as public information) I'm sure that information just shocked you!

One of the ways to hedge our business is to be aware of what is happening on a worldwide scale, but do not over-react if the news is unfavorable. Subscribe to an unbiased and trustworthy channel or website and keep abreast of the latest news, always thinking of how your business can benefit, or needed preparations to guard your cash flow. You can check out my favorite site: NewsNow.com. This site is phenomenal because I don't have to waste time on news stories that don't apply to me and my business. This particular news source is the alpha of sources where news happens first before word gets out around the world. As entrepreneurs, we need to take an active approach to newsworthy stories and always look at the positive side, believing in possibilities and opportunities.

Lack of Industry Necessity: Finding an industry's value is the key to knowing if you have a winning product or service to market within a specific area. Analyzing similar regions can give you answers as well as the status of a community's economy. Be broad-minded in your deductions. Just because a community doesn't have many dry cleaners doesn't mean it doesn't want one. Perhaps no one has ever opened such a business in the area. In our search, there were awnings on shopping center storefronts, restaurant patios, and hotel entrances. However, there was only a couple of awning companies here. Shortly after moving to the area, we discovered that a long-time company had gone out of business due to the owner retiring and his children not wanting to continue the family business. We landed in a prime area to open our awning company! Also, since we moved here, there has been an enormous migration south as political uncertainty and high taxes in some states have forced Americans to look for stability elsewhere. Being at the right place at the right time in history as it unfolds is where the real magic happens.

Low Market Demand: To determine the need for any particular item or service, you need to analyze who your customer is and the likelihood they will purchase from you. For instance, if you are an expensive car importer, the chances of you having multiple sales in a rural farming community aren't too great. Contact your local Chamber of Commerce or Business Alliance group if you have trouble finding per capita numbers of consumer purchases or local support. They often have annual, if not quarterly, breakdowns of goods and services. You can also speak with industry business owners or Commercial Real Estate groups to see how many businesses are failing or growing within a specific area. Again, you want to ensure a high demand for your business before sinking your life savings into an endeavor. Here's one funny, but sad story I heard in a marketing class years ago I never forgot: Many years ago, Chevy made a car model called a Nova. They wanted to expand their reach into an untapped market south of the border-Mexico. Without doing any research on the name of the car or how it would impact sales, they moved forward with opening a dealership in the area. Not one Chevy Nova sold. Why? Because in Spanish, the name means "doesn't run". Remember that fools rush in, wisdom steps cautiously.

HIGH COMPETITION: If an area has several high-quality widget makers, chances are, none of them will have a thriving business unless one or two offer some specialty or consistent advertising. There are only so many people in any given area to support any given product or service. But, if your competition sells poor quality or there is no competition at all, then the chances of your success increase dramatically. Because an industry can be competitive on price points, several companies will have to downgrade their products to compete in the marketplace. The basic economic foundation of supply and demand drives prices of products and services down, resulting in companies going out of business. Try to stay away from the high competition if at all possible.

IN SOME AREAS, you won't see a single awning, and in other areas, you'll see them on just about every home or business. Some awnings will be of inferior quality, while others are top-of-the-line gorgeous. A great way to determine if your awning business or other subcontracting business will succeed in a geographical area, find out about the demographics of its residents. The higher the income levels of the residents, the higher their expectations are of aesthetically prone storefronts. You can make a sizable amount of money with little effort by doing market research and being open to where the business has potential. But, as we've discussed, there are more steps to determine if a market is worthy of your business.

BEFORE LAUNCHING into a marketing campaign in your 'presumed' ideal market, make sure you are ready for the big times. Your business can hit fast and hard, and being prepared for this will build your image and reputation with respect and admiration.

#1. **Start Small.** Stay focused on your foundation. If you move forward with too many jobs before you know how the first few are progressing, you'll lose quality control and may be out of business before receiving your first payout.

ALWAYS ASK FOR A 50% deposit before the commencement of the project. By doing this, you'll still be able to keep the business going without risking the entire profit on the customers' final payment. A deposit also invests the customer in the project, lessening the possibility of not honoring the contract. Be realistic about what your company can achieve and what it's not ready to take on.

#2. **Work Smart.** The awning and shade industry is a long-term type of business. It requires your commitment to working five days a week with at least a 3-hour a day focused dedication until you find employees to fill your roles. If you learn to organize your time to work each day efficiently, you will undoubtedly become successful. Develop a duplicatable system from the beginning so you can transition out of all the hats you might be wearing in this business. If you can't do it yourself, hire someone else.

#3 BE DIGITAL MARKETING SAVVY. Your online presence is often the first thing a potential client will see of your business, either on their handheld device (phone most likely), tablet, or computer. Make sure your website is formatted to each device so all information will show up clearly and legibly. A rule to judge your site by: If the customer can't see your product, is unclear of your process, can't find the answer to their question, or isn't able to find a way to contact you, then they will move on to your competition, end of story. If your website is of poor quality, you've just handed your competition a customer, and the money which should have been in your pocket will be in theirs. Do your homework and find a reputable site host and designer to create a website for you if you are challenged in this area.

ON THE OTHER HAND, don't be discouraged if hiring a designer is out of your budget. Most site hosts, such as GoDaddy, DreamHost, GreenGeeks, and A2 Hosting, are popular hosting services (modern platforms, quality performance, priced reasonably, no downtime, and offers 24/7 customer support) with options for designing the site yourself or links to a plethora of sites (such as WordPress). As I mentioned earlier, our favorite is GoDaddy for several reasons. They are not perfect, but they are perfect for us.

When searching, keep an eye on their Better Business Bureau ratings and what TrustPilot has to say. It's better to get more information than you need here, as you will rely on your website more than you could ever imagine.

Everyone has their own opinion on who the best is, but we found GoDaddy to work well. We designed our own site, CanvasBackAwnings.com, for under $200 per year, and the service has been excellent. Your host most likely will provide you with many additional goodies such as email addresses, campaign bots, analysis, etc... Utilizing these processes take some time to develop, but they will ultimately improve your business revenue over the long haul. Take time to research the most modern website templates offered and how they benefit your needs and industry. Remember that your potential client is probably internet savvy and can distinguish between a good website and an outdated one. A website should be treated as your professional "elevator pitch," as sales gurus will tell you in their popular books. You have one chance to make a great impression on the potential client. By making these critical decisions, you can see if having someone else design your site or D.I.Y. will be most cost-effective.

Be Organized

Successful entrepreneurs will tell you to make a plan for the week in addition to a daily plan. List the three most important tasks for the week and then the three most important tasks per day. The rest of your tasks can be listed under those. Eventually, extra tasks make it to the top three on the list due to the organization, the focus of each task, and your ease in completing the listed goals. Give it some time to develop this habit. Soon, you'll recognize that you are benefiting from this plan. I do certain tasks on specific days and sometimes during specific hours. By doing this, you can become proactive and resist the temptation of working in a reactive mode. If you don't stay committed to your schedule, you will quickly find yourself blown around like a leaf in the wind. You need to devise a plan and stick with it. Think your routine through and then move forward with a plan.

IF YOU FEEL the middle of the week gives you a bit of breathing time, schedule sales calls on Wednesday. Clients are often more apt to listen intently to you as the week slows down after a busy Monday. You may also find, as I did, that toward the end of the day is an excellent time to schedule appointments, as the 'gate-keeper' has gone home and the owner most often answers the phone. You not only have the appointment, but you've also made contact with the decision-maker and had the opportunity to develop your relationship with them.

COMMUNICATIONS: just the word can send chills through a C.E.O.'s veins or send the most competent marketer running for the door. But you don't have to be afraid of it; confidence and training will cure your fears. Communications can be the most rewarding part of your business. In any outsourcing business, communication is a necessity:

1. It's how you gain, retain, and further develop your client base.

2. It's how you achieve organization on projects.
3. It's how you stay on top of your business, even when your orders triple and your personal life expands.

A Day at the Shop

We talked about being organized when your business launches. Here, I'm going to spell out how a business schedule would look in our office.

Daily Tasks:

- Answer incoming calls
- Answer all current client's emails and correspondence right away.
- Forward new project leads from your email inbox into a master list.
- Respond to leads immediately with a scripted automatic message or phone call (recommended) listing your business contact information as a "signature" (found in settings of your email provider).
- Enter lead contact with description to Master Quote List

Throughout the Week:

- Follow up on quotes sent from last week's list.

Schedule list for appointments with clients at the location of the project
- Forward any tasks to other employees who may need inclusion or support
- Visit the client's office for final payment checks or arrange closeout of the projects.
- Order supplies from vendors (try to combine orders to lower your shipping costs)
- Schedule jobs with contractors, follow up on current orders (sewers, contractors, installers)

Emails and other Communications

Because emails play a large part in communication, use these tips to make sure your communications are understood and helpful:

- Keep emails short, concise, and very personable. Always type a heading in the subject line, so the customer will know it's from you, such as 'Awning Bid for July Install' or such. (use *Urgent* for current clients)

- Use complete sentences and words with proper grammar. Don't abbreviate unless it's of universal use. (Grammarly is a great tool for correcting mistakes)

- Ensure your signature includes your contact information: phone number, website link, and a business card photo image added.

GET A BRAND LOGO: Your business profile grows as your logo becomes recognizable. Design your own for free at Canva.com or have someone else design a logo for you on Upwork.com or 99designs.com. Don't let designing a logo hold up your invoicing or your website launch. It's essential, but it can't stand in the way of progress. Insert your logo on every document and communication tool you use; website pages, URL address, business cards, email signatures (if appropriate), and financial documents (invoices, statements, tax reports, etc.). Your professional logo is your brand that imprints your business image into the minds of your target market (and Google loves a photo image as a logo). but graphic images work well also. It is the most basic memory 'stamp' the brain uses. (be aware of copyright laws) Simple works best, and keep in mind that colors may show up differently in print than online. Only change it if your logo is outdated in design style or your company is well-established. With these details in mind, design away!

JOB-STATUS BOARDS: If you need to keep even just a few team members updated on the progress of orders and jobs, it will be helpful to purchase a large dry-erase board or some other medium of keeping updates visible. Many businesses rely on this simple technique, and often it has been the most measurable means of current information. For record-keeping purposes, take a snapshot of it before erasing it.

. . .

Join industry groups: The Industrial Fabrics Association International I F A I is the largest association for awning companies. It has proven its value time and again in supplying information and connections with other awning companies with new products and services for industry growth. Imagine that as a goal for your business! Your company can become an industry leader and end up with your photo on its cover magazine.

Your Clients Determine Your Profits

I have found that incredibly successful people have one thing in common throughout my years in business. I have mentioned it before, but I don't think it can be repeated enough.

The respect you have for your clients and the integrity you exhibit as a business person will rise above any high-end marketing scheme or latest awning design. If you never take your clients for granted and build a strong network in your community, then your company will be the first on their minds when they are ready for your product and service. Having a business with a consistently positive reputation is priceless, and it begins with your very first order. Follow the simple suggestions laid out in this book, and the rest of your business plans will naturally follow, providing the client with a memorable business profile.

Summary

Thorough research on your target market is a necessity before opening your doors for business. Once you begin, stay on top of your industry.

Use outside support to handle tasks you are not capable of doing or are not economically wise. Handle daily tasks with efficiency and duplicatable systems in place.

Establish a professional presence online with a recognizable logo and website.

Treating your customers with respect and professionalism goes a long way in determining if your business will become profitable in the long term.

In the next chapter, we will go deeper into successful strategies concerning time management, streamlining your processes, and some other secrets we've learned.

Notes:

_____
_____
_____
_____
_____

5

TOOLS FOR YOUR SUCCESS

"If you really want to do something, you'll find a way. If you don't, you'll find an excuse."
~ Jim Rohn

You will find out soon (as we did), some unconventional methods will make your business function at a higher efficiency rate, keeping your mind calm and your personal life untethered. You want it all, right? I don't think you are giving up a 9 to 5 job that milks your inner-self dry only to trade it in for an owner-run business that keeps you working 24/7!

It's important to have some balance between your personal life and business by having support teams and backup in place to keep you sleeping well at night and your spouse happy on the weekends.

Being a business owner is more than just making your schedule and developing a price list. It includes keeping a management plan functional and using leadership skills to guide the path to your goals. You need to do what other companies are unwilling to do, or do what other companies too big to care will not do if you want to stand out.

Time is $$$ Valuable

Be early for all appointments with clients. It's worth noting that integrity begins with respecting your client's time. Remember, The Golden Rule is: "Treat others how you would want them to treat you." Easy enough, right? By letting this fundamental rule sink into your mind, you will retain the customers you initially attract. People enjoy doing business with consistent, respectable companies that go above and beyond to ensure their clients' needs are met with sensitivity. You will profit significantly from the foundational business ethics of old-school entrepreneurs like us because, for some weird reason, integrity is hard to find these days.

To run a fully functional outsourcing business, I've found certain items that need to be in place. I've streamlined the process through the years and used backup techniques for every possible scenario we may face in the awning business. Below is a comprehensive list:

- Keep all documents in a file on your desktop for convenience.
- Keep your list of quotes organized by Contact Date.
- File invoices by Completion Date, then sort to the Finished file when completed.
- Keep Call Sheets for new calls on a clipboard at all times.
- Begin a Budget Sheet with each order
- Have an Invoice template in place, with all possible items listed (as well as blank spaces for miscellaneous)
- Make Quote forms simple and easily understood for the customer.
- Transfer all email information (from lead) to Call sheet and Contact List/Database
- Keep a file on your desktop for documents you will need for every job, such as W.C. exempt forms, W-9, shipping courier information, etc.
- Collect 50% down payment for all jobs before ordering materials. No exceptions!
- And make sure everyone gets their breaks, including you!

Financial Business Smarts

Establishing your business credit takes time, and your personal credit score weighs into these factors in the beginning. Some choose to take out a business loan to establish a credit history by paying it back quickly. This method establishes your institutional financial relationship in addition to giving you a cushion if the need for extra cash becomes critical. If you are using your own money to launch your business, make sure your C.P.A. or accountant is aware of your actions and advises you through the spending. Deduct everything possible; otherwise, your taxes will skyrocket without a thing for you to show.

EXAMPLE: Instead of paying $14,000 in taxes for the year, your business can purchase a vehicle and write off the purchase as a deduction. Make sure your accountant guides you through the process before you jump into any assumptions. This strategy is called "tax planning."

SAFEGUARDING your business cash flow is also an essential part of your business's financial profile. New business owners often tend to use their personal accounts when paying for business items, which causes problems when filing your taxes. Always separate personal accounts from business accounts. Imagine if you can't finish a project because the client's deposit was spent on something else! Save for a rainy day in business in the same way as you save for your family's emergency fund, but be aware of Uncle Sam's tactics in squeezing every dime from your business savings. You'll want to have payroll for several months on hand if you have employees, as well as operational funding and purchases.

I TALKED EARLIER about purchasing insurance which helps cover emergencies. Doing so will keep you from risking business loss when the economy dips or supplies become scarce. By weathering such economic hardships, you will also be the first company customers will come to when business picks back up again, keeping you at the forefront and restating your business savvy and staying power.

Our Business Secrets

Finding New Business: If you find yourself with some extra time, drive through your city. We loved to take Sunday morning drives because no one else was on the road. Pay close attention to the awning and shade structures on businesses and apartment buildings, homes, and community structures (libraries and schools). Notice what structures need repair, cleaning, or replacement, and don't be afraid to take lots of pictures for referrals and ideas.

Also, notice buildings that could use a shade structure but don't have one. Take pictures of these also, as well as writing down the address and business name. Research who manages the property or the names on the lease (check the local Chamber of Commerce or county public records if necessary). If you have a specific type of awning that would look good on their building, do a line-over-photo drawing or use the Awning Composer program and insert the proposal with a letter of introduction. Mention you would like to make an appointment to discuss your suggestions and follow up your introduction letter with a phone call. The worst thing they could do is say 'no.' And the best thing would be if they hire you to do the job! This plan works well for homes and business structures alike. Maybe a snow cone shack standing in the middle of a hot parking lot or a small coffee bar or restaurant could use an excellent shade structure.

. . .

THE LIST GOES on and on. Once you get going, you will see awnings could be part of every business front, and you'd be right! Just make sure the businesses you contact have the means to purchase the design, or you'll be wasting your time. Some areas you "may" waste time would be abandoned buildings, churches, car washes, and laundry facilities. Feel out the potential client with questions about when they will be interested in purchasing. If they don't have a clear answer, then probably not for some time.

BESIDES THE DRIVE-BY shooting photos on a Sunday morning, another great way to market directly to the potential client is to do a web search for property management or realty companies in your area and email them your contact information. When we began our business, we would find the contact number on the website of nearby companies who could use our services, and call them for their email address. Let them know your company is now expanded to the area, and you would like to send over your company profile for their files in case they might need your services. It's not intrusive or "pitchy" to do this method of direct marketing. This process takes some time but is well worth the trouble. We have made mega money this way in the beginnings of our business.

OUTSOURCING: When beginning your business, you won't have sewers, manufacturers, or installers. Before you open your doors, these skilled laborers must be in place, ready to work. You can operate fully by contracting the entire project and getting your profit percentage when the final check comes. But there are several steps you'll want to complete before you sign any contracts with vendors:

#1 FIND **a sewer to make your awnings:** Without an experienced sewer in awning manufacturing, either contracted or hourly, you won't have a business, which pretty much doesn't require anyone else down the pipeline, of course. You can place ads for sewing technicians in local papers and community newsletters. Contact trade associations, or speak with your awning representative and suppliers. You can also get in touch with other awning businesses to see if they would be interested in manufacturing your projects for a set price. Often, when these shops aren't too busy, they look to other businesses to supplement their expenses. Search the internet for awning businesses nearest your chosen business location, but also check out other areas you might find a manufacturer. Think of areas that may use sewers and check to see if they hire their services out. If you don't find anyone nearby, a contracted sewer can be anywhere. All you need is exact measurements of the awning to be constructed and send them through an email to your sewing contractor. You can also drop-ship the fabric supplies directly to the contractor if that is the arrangement. After you have a contact or two:

- Check samples for quality and safety compliance during the interview.
- Make sure all other business operations are in order.
- Don't associate with a business just because they happen to do what you need.

- Ensure it's up to your standards because this is your own company's work as far as the client is concerned.

#2 FIND A GOOD WELDER: What is valid with sewers is also true with fabricators. Search out welders and make sure you see other work they've done. Test bead strength if possible, and get referrals from past jobs. If you need to hire a fabricator, make sure the business is reputable and not someone's job on the side. Again, your name is on the work. Make sure it's the best you can provide. Here's a Tip: You don't need a welder to start your company. You can be an awning company that only manufactures the fabric covers and keep it that simple. You will get more projects with a welding fabricator, obviously, but it's not a must.

#3 TEST A JOB IF POSSIBLE: Of course, this would be the ideal situation to see if these workers are up to your needs and standards. Have them test samples for you with your requested dimensions and specifics. Repeat this process until you find the people you need.

#4 MAKE SURE Your Digital Marketing Has a Successful Response: By using Google Analytics (or other analytics software used by your site host), you can see where your marketing is working and where it might need a bit of help. Mastering this process isn't hard, but SEO is a time-consuming task, and putting together a digital presence and campaign can take the average person months to complete.

Take small bite-size chunks of time to add more strength to your digital marketing strategies if you do it yourself. Know the words to search for to find the information you are looking for, such as 'keywords for awning business,' 'writing website copy for an awning business, or 'free pictures to use'. As I mentioned earlier, often your web hosting company will offer you these services as well. Check into Fivver.com or Upwork.com if you would like to hire someone to do this for you.

#5 SCHEDULE **Specific Tasks After Hours:** There are specific tasks that you must do during the business day, such as talking to clients, discussing orders with sub-contractors, and having meetings with business associates. Other tasks can be handled after hours, as long as you schedule them into your work week and make sure you aren't burning the candle at both ends. Owning your own business doesn't mean you work twice as hard for half as much pay!

SOME OF THE tasks we schedule for after-hours include:

- Entering financial data (invoices, receivables, and payables)
- Answering emails that were by-passed earlier
- Assemble digital ad campaigns on social media (or write a blog)
- Uploading photos into project files (Devise a workable file naming system to keep photocopies searchable for future reference)
- Training and education courses (online)

- Posting on social media
- Project quotes that you didn't finish during the day.

IF YOU KEEP to your schedule and prioritize your work tasks, you can get most jobs done during the workday. If not, however, some need to be delegated to the 'after hours' category.

Financial Rules to Live By

When borrowing money, most people think about monthly payments rather than the entire sum of things. This kind of thinking is dangerous for the entrepreneur. Instead, think along these lines:

- What is the initial cost of the item?
- How much is the total interest over the life of the loan?
- What is my Return on Investment (or R.O.I.)? (The amount of time it takes to get your investment back)

IF YOU FEEL you aren't financially savvy, enroll in a finance class or online business course. The cost of time and money will pay you back in the long-term. Education is a critical endeavor to become successful in business, and you must keep learning. One tidbit of information you will learn in finance is this: Most financial products have an amortization schedule, which means your interest payments are highest at the beginning of any loan; eventually the principal payment becomes the more significant portion of the loan payment over time. Plainly speaking, the bank wants its interest first. For this reason, it is worth mentioning to use caution when considering a loan.

Credit Score and Ratings

Yes, you have a business credit score (or will have), and no, they don't work quite like your own personal credit score and credit report. Initially, your financial institution may pull a credit history, but they look for payment maintenance and account history. If your company is not yet established, your business credit score won't be established either. Before building business credit, your personal credit must be exemplary. Below is a list of tips to raise your Personal Credit Score in record time:

ALWAYS REMEMBER that with even one negative mark on your credit, your score can drop by 100 points in some cases. Many factors can lower your score, late payments, collections, high debt, too many pulls on credit score, and the list goes on. However, there are only a few ways to raise it. Take action with the suggestions below:

- Your credit purchases must not go higher than 30% of the limit.
- Never pay late on loans or credit. Set a minimum auto pay if necessary just to keep this unfortunate scenario from happening

- Never close credit cards once opened.
- Make the most significant payment on the highest balance first
- Ask for an increase in credit lines to increase the credit limit and the charged ratio gap.
- If you have a Home Equity Line of Credit (HELOC), ask the lender to report it as a mortgage. (installment vs. revolving)

Long History of Credit Accounts:

- Accounts older than five years with a limit of more than five thousand credit limit are considered "most secure," which positively impacts your score.
- Use the old accounts that you keep inactive to pay off open balances once a year.
- Become an "authorized user" on a family member's older account with a high limit if possible. This method is called "piggybacking" on someone else's credit.

New Credit

- Four major credit cards within two years should be the goal.
- Do not allow mail offers for credit to come to your mailbox. Go to www.optoutprescreen.com and print the authorization page, sign, and mail

it. Opting out of receiving credit approvals by mail will be permanent, and the credit bureau rewards you with a 10 point increase within 45 days of notice.
- Don't open consumer credit cards such as Target, Dillards, Walmart. If you already have store cards, don't close them, but don't use any except once a year to keep them active. Closing accounts will negatively impact your credit score.

THE GOAL IS to raise your credit score and keep it there for several reasons. Generally, it's harder to get a loan when you own a small business because instead of providing a check stub from a job for proof of income, you will most likely need tax returns from previous years and profit and loss statements for the current year. Of course, you can always pay yourself large paychecks by being on the payroll, but in the beginning when your business is in its infant stage, this may not be a good idea. The reality is this: As an entrepreneurial taxpayer, you will deduct everything, or your taxes will be high. So to the loan officer, it will look like you don't make any money with your business. The choice is, "Do I pay boatloads of money to the I.R.S. so that I can get that loan?" the answer could be yes or no. Tax planning and loan planning ahead of time is essential to the entrepreneur for this reason. If you always pay attention to your credit score, you can save thousands of dollars in interest over time.

. . .

THERE ARE three credit bureaus for businesses: Dun & Bradstreet, Equifax, and Experian. Just as personal credit reports, transactions are compiled to give financial institutions a report of a business' credit profile and eligibility for credit products, including credit cards, lines of credit, and loans. Your business credit report includes:

- Historical data of your business, such as the date you opened for business and when your business license was issued
- Details on business registration
- Operational data for your business
- Company demographics: employee count, sales, ownership, and any attached business or subsidiaries
- A government summary of activity
- Industry class and data
- All public notices and fillings, including liens, judgments, and U.C.C. filings
- Account reports details (number of accounts, names on accounts, etc.)
- Past payment history and any collections
- The Small Business Association (S.B.A.) also includes information on
- Supplier amounts of credit extended to the business
- The amount credit or financial institutions will lend to you.
- The repayment terms of credit lending
- The interest rates of any credit lent.
- Customer remarks of your business
- Insurance premium amount you incur

THOUGH BUSINESS SCORES use similar means for calculating as personal scores do, the models for the results are different, being pulled by two leading agencies, Dun & Bradstreet PAYDEX Score and Experian Intelliscore Plus. Scores range from 1 to 100, with a higher number indicating a better score. Score models weigh your payment history, age of accounts, amount of debt, and the balances on your credit compared to allowed amounts. A missed payment, overextended credit, etc., are also recorded and weighs the score.

RETRIEVING your business credit score is a bit more complicated than finding your consumer score. Some are marketed as 'free' but often don't include many finer points a business score supplies, painting an incomplete picture. Below is a list of low-cost or free options to keep track of your business scores and protection against fraud:

DUN & BRADSTREET Credit Signal

- Notices when your score and ratings change
- A monthly summary of all activity in your business credit record
- Notices of how often your file is accessed
- You won't receive access to your full Dun & Bradstreet business credit report and credit score for free. You'll need to pay for the upgrade to CreditBuilder Plus per month (the least expensive credit subscription).

Nav Business Credit Report

- A summary of the Dun & Bradstreet, Experian, and Equifax business credit report
- Business credit grades for each score, including your personal Experian credit score
- Many helpful tools to build your business credit score
- You won't receive the complete reports of any of the credit bureaus reports free, but you can upgrade to the Nav Business Manager, with the ability to report errors on each report.

BELOW ARE two more credit report choices, and vary with price and what's offered. You can go to their websites and see the different options and costs for their packages.

3. **Experian Business Credit Report**
4. **Equifax Business Credit Report**

Summary

Time is valuable to the entrepreneur. Learning to streamline your process is key to becoming financially free in the future of your business.

GET knowledgeable with financial matters regarding your business ventures, taxes, and loans. If you can save, say, $100k from tax debt, interest, or overpaying for supplies, would you do it?

. . .

A GOOD BUSINESS credit score is essential for maintaining a healthy business during lean times. Business loans used wisely can keep you from shutting down if cash flow is low and unexpected circumstances occur.

HAVING a prepared plan for meeting a 5-year business credit goal gives you a strategy to accomplish more as a business owner when you can seize an opportunity through creditworthiness.

IN THE NEXT CHAPTER, you will learn how to win customers over your competition.

NOTES:

_____
_____
_____
_____
_____
_____
_____
_____
_____
_____

6

SCORING OVER YOUR COMPETITION

"Your significance is not in your similarity to another, but in your point of difference from another." ~ Mike Murdock

By now, I'm sure you might feel like you have a pretty good handle on the awning industry (or your chosen business industry). There are still gems of wisdom and logic to be found! Though this confidence builds within you, don't begin taking action steps until you've read to the end of this book. Stay with me here for a couple more chapters, because throughout the end of this book, you'll see how to implement what you've learned and turned it into your business.

Industry Competition

A little competition is good to have in a market; it keeps businesses striving for betterment while still keeping them honest with the patrons they serve. And as a business person yourself, you will also stay on the top of your game and offer fantastic products. If you knew someone could come along and take the money right out of your hand, you would always stay on top of your game.

Though you will quickly find out who your main competitors are when you open your business doors, you may never see the owners face to face or come in contact with their employees. But this doesn't mean you won't know every move they make or each campaign they launch. Even if you keep your eyes closed, you'll have a natural pulse on the industry around you just by searching out clients and listening to their needs. Quite often, it will be your clients who give you the most information about your competitors. And the news won't be about how wonderful they believe your competition is treating them!

"Try not to become a man of success, but rather try to become a man of value." ~ Albert Einstein

Impeccable Service = High Profits

I can't stress the importance of having a solid and reputable client-business relationship that will speak volumes to buyers and be the thorn in your competitors' side (even if they have just as good of product). By establishing integrity when you sign your first contract with a client (a set of rules for yourself and your team to follow), you will have sewn up the market on outstanding services.

IN OUR BUSINESS, we believe in it so much that we offer a package for our clients that will keep us coming back to service their purchase and keep it looking clean, new, and functioning perfectly for the duration of the product. We want them to be happier with their purchase five years down the road than they are the day we finish their job and drive away. We want them to know we believe in our products so much that we are willing to return year after year to keep those awnings looking good and serving a purpose. Along with providing a fantastic product, you must also give your customers the satisfaction that you will be there to take care of them if they need anything. Beginning with the first 'hello' of the relationship, continuing for the duration of the company. Many people buy on this confidence alone, just knowing they won't be left with a product that may fail or not perform as promised. You appreciate it as a consumer; give your clients the same appreciation you want.

EVERY CLIENT DESERVES a pre-construction package if there is a large project to be completed. They will appreciate the meticulous details spelled out for clarity since most clients are unfamiliar with the process. Extras such as this are considered above and beyond the competition. (details on this later)

Attend Networking Events

Though advertising your business is essential, you can find massive business in the back doors of contractor meetings with the city and county planning committees, as well as local township zoning meetings and permit notifications. When you find a new application for a zoning permit or town hall meeting, sit in on the meetings (most are open to the public) and send your brochure or make an appointment to speak with the contractor for design needs. If there are shops, porches, patios, or gathering places, chances are, there will be a need for shade structures and awnings too.

There are also many other ways to stay connected to the business community in your area. Consider joining any local trade associations, Chamber of Commerce, chapters, leagues, rotaries, and other clubs. Not only will you be making connections with other businesses, but often, these associations will need your services too!

Now, do you see why I don't want you to answer phones? You need to focus on growing, not menial tasks, which will get you nowhere but frustrated down the road.

Expert Marketing Tips

If there is ever an industry that has flooded the internet with programs, methods, strategies, and courses, it is marketing. You can invest as little as $7 or as much as $15,000 to gain knowledge and stake a claim at being a marketing genius. However, if you are like we were initially, you don't have thousands of dollars to spend on ideas, strategies, and guerrilla marketing excesses.

Hopefully, when you were reading the previous chapters, the suggestions made sense to you. If your awning or outsourcing company serves only commercial properties, chances are you will never have a face-to-face meeting with the client. However, word of mouth will begin to spread from the first few jobs because of the smooth process you have created for the client who took a chance on you. Soon you'll be handling a lucrative and busy office.

A wise advertising genius once said:

"For every dollar you spend on advertising, spend one dollar on quality control. Let your product speak volumes where your ad dollars cannot."

And that means word of mouth.

Digital and Social Media Campaigns

I've mentioned how a website can connect you to your potential clients and positive emails and blogs to keep the relationship strong with your current clients. How do you build confidence in a client's mind when you are a one-person show trying to line up the best sewing contractors and fabricators? You become the industry expert: Learn your industry as much as possible, and you will know more than your clients.

When speaking to clients, pretend you are in their position and speak in terms they understand, offering to help them with their problems. If you throw around industry jargon, it goes right over their heads and makes you seem arrogant, so don't do that! Over and over again, I listened to clients tell me that the other companies' salespeople weren't answering their needs and acted pompous with their knowledge. They wanted us to do the job because we were knowledgeable but also compassionate.

The Stanford Research Institute says that the money you make in any endeavor is determined only 12.5 percent by knowledge and 87.5 percent by your ability to deal with people. (Maxwell 2010)

87.5% people knowledge + 12.5% product knowledge = SUCCESS

If you struggle with sales or communicating with people, you are not among a few. Books and videos are available to learn techniques that will help you 'close the deal'. I recommend starting with my favorite mentor, Kevin McArdle. You can watch his videos for free on YouTube. It's not complicated to learn from him, just trust that his methods work.

. . .

REMEMBER, your company is the solution to their problem. There are many ways to connect to your clients, but they often won't know you until they need your services. Your potential client will search online to see who you are and what you do. A first impression is a lasting impression. Your website should have the edge they are looking for by having an established reputation, even if only a few articles about the quality of your products and some personal interests can be general but compelling (think animal passions, non-profit volunteering, or family activities). Give your readers some cozy information about yourself or your business, making them feel like they know you or have commonalities with you. It's what separates you from the competition, even if their products are as good as yours. The general perception of your company should be that you're not afraid to engage your audience. Engagement is what readers of blog posts want, give them that, and they'll spread your good name like wildfire (for free). Always link your posts back to your website or a page on your site directly tied to the post. Never pass up this free connection!

LET me expand on each platform to give you some ideas for posting short and exciting messages.

LINKEDIN - THIS PLATFORM is our favorite for connecting clients in the B2B sector. Create a page for your business, relaying how your business started, services you offer, why you are a business owner, and what makes each day extraordinary for you. In LinkedIn, you can post articles to your network for free, so pick an area of your industry and write a brief, informative piece, either sharing an experience, sharing a common like of the industry, or telling a client's story (with their permission, of course). We found that sharing tidbits of knowledge on fabric choices, what to look for in choosing a company, or keeping the price lower when purchasing gives the reader something to smile about. Keep it light, short, enjoyable, and positive. Post consistently and often (once a week is fine here). Soon, you will develop a readership, and as one topic leads to another, your chain of connectivity builds to gathering contacts and more relationships. You can follow groups such as Property Management, Contractors, Architects, City Councils, etc. Always add new connections to your network. When we started out, we added connections daily to our network, reaching thousands of members. LinkedIn will make suggestions of people and companies to connect with, so utilize their free services. As your connections grow, so will your business. Learn to make the most of every opportunity to gain another customer. Always post quality images and positive content. Link this back to your website, always!

FACEBOOK PAGE - If you serve the general public, Facebook will be a valuable tool for free advertising. You can show a short clip of an installation, a panorama of a final product, before and after photos, or an introduction to a client who hosts a grand opening of their business. Again, keep it light, enjoyable, and positive. And again, insert a link to your website or another social media piece with a common idea. Your F.B. business page is an extension of your personal profile on F.B. as an administrator of your "business page." You have the choice of opening up a comments option or not. Most times, comments will build your business, but sometimes they won't. If you allow it, you must make time to respond. Consider this choice wisely.

Another piece of advice I want to mention is that Facebook has the most definitive marketing strategies, it's quite scary what they know about us. However, you can use this powerful strategy in your favor. When you place your ads, you can narrow your ad to a specific group of people who would be interested in your product, and the price is cheap as of this writing. Create a "lead magnet" to get them to your business page, and then you can message each one or use an ad campaign mail response system. We never needed a mail response system in our business, but it's worth mentioning here for those who want to take it to the next level. I cannot advise on mail systems because I am just now beginning to get familiar with the need for it as an author.

INSTAGRAM - THIS IS a great medium to share photos of your work from your cellphone. Use photos with lots of color and variety. Remember, your picture is competing for 'views' of other pictures and images. Make yours the one they choose to click on and post. And then? Link it to your website and other social media. Reminder: Watermark all photos before uploading! Be sure to share information in short sentence posts and make sure your client approves any images you post of clients' shops.

PINTEREST - MEDIA IS similar to Instagram, though users can store your pictures in categories with similar photos. Very visual, very easy to use, including linking back to associated material. If you decide to invest advertising dollars on any media choices, Pinterest is the least expensive. You can also specify your audience a bit easier in the tutorials. Again, pick clear, colorful, and exciting photos of your work. What catches the eye might be the bait for your next big project.

YOUTUBE - PODCASTS, videos, and how-to shorts are becoming the best way to get your information out. They are casual, to the point, entertaining, and addictive. If you are comfortable in front of a camera, shoot some videos and post them. These are becoming more and more popular with customers. Keep the videos under 8 minutes, half that or less if you think of using them as an ad. Information bombardment can turn off a potential client just as quickly as it can turn them on. Use your best judgment, and consider what you would like to see in a video of your business. What can the viewer learn from your video? List the URL address on your website and link it up to your YouTube channel. An effective video presentation can be before and after photos, instruction on the purchase process from ordering a quote to completion of the project, a commercial advertisement, or a fast forward beginning to end installation.

TWITTER - If your followers want to share in every moment of your business life, Twitter is the place to be. It may have been created for celebrities initially because they use it constantly. However, posting photos of completed work is free, so you may find it helpful. The downside of this media is that it will only be seen a short time, so to rectify this time span problem, you can add tags to your posts so your "followers" will get a notification. Also, you must keep your message short and to the point. There is no way around it, but if you add a link to another page, that would be recommended to explain any details you may need to focus on. Check it out and decide if you could utilize this method of advertisement.

ALL OF THESE social media platforms sell advertising, so you can have an ad rotating for your local or national regions. Many also have 'followers' interested in your company and will be notified when you post new messages, such as a new product launch or when you have specials and sales. If you decide to spend a budget on advertising, use your advertising dollars wisely. At the beginning of our business, we wasted too much money on useless ad campaigns just too embarrassing to talk about. Start with the free and cheap to see how well it works for you before making a costly decision. Then you can scale up by spending small amounts and tracking the ads. It's imperative to keep track of which advertising is getting you the most business, free or not.

DON'T BE afraid to use these platforms for your business. They have instructional tutorials on each site, and if you are still confused, go to YouTube and find a video you like to explain the details that interest you.

A WORD TO THE WISE: If you don't have time to post on different sites, use all of these platforms anyway, even if you don't like the social media arena. Just take the time to set them all up, and you can use Hootsuite.com to connect them all into one post that shoots out to all platforms if you like or focus on one at a time. The choice is yours. Remember that it's all electricity to power your website and your company, and this is why we recommend using all of them.

IF YOU ONLY LISTEN TO one reason why you should, let it be this - It's free advertising! Not to mention Google will appreciate your effort by listing your company on the first page of a search keyword "awnings in 'fill in the blank'" You can rest assured that your competition is using social media. If you don't, you'll soon be following the tail of the lead dog in your industry.

THIS BOOK TEACHES lots of money-making ideas to implement on how to market your company for zero dollars. The author has a strong background in marketing, even before the partnership began in our awning business many years ago, so I enjoy performing these tasks myself as a business owner, leaving the rest of the work to other skilled professionals. If you are still in doubt of your marketing and advertising skills after reading *"the Secret Online Business,"* look to the internet for online help in any specific subject I've listed if you wish. You may find a few people whose ideas you are drawn to and follow them and their advice.

IF I WAS EVER STUCK on stupid in trying to accomplish a task, I would go directly to the website that had the answers. I would spend an evening immersing myself in watching their videos and/or read the script. When you are short on time, you can even email or call the support line for faster help.

Summary

Don't be afraid of a bit of competition with other companies in your industry. You'll be more likely to stay on top of your game. Give your potential clients a good reason to choose you for their next project.

Stay in the loop with community events and city council projects. You will gain insight and memorable connections in networking to grow your business.

Make your website the go-to element for your business when you aren't available. It should answer questions, give information, provide a way to be contacted, and depict an air of your personality.

Always use links and contact info in your online pages and posts. They give you an image of being an expert in your industry and increase traffic to your site.

Use social media with positive, engaging, and entertaining information. Keep your personal life separate from business by creating a business page.

. . .

In the next chapter, you will learn leadership and team management, discussing how your business can grow by assembling a team of competent self-starters who can follow your lead.

Notes:

_____
_____
_____
_____
_____
_____
_____
_____
_____
_____

7

NECESSITIES FOR GROWTH

"A man's mind, stretched by a new idea,
can never go back to its original dimension."
~ Oliver Wendell Holmes

One prevalent situation I find to be the reason some small businesses get stuck in a rut and stay mediocre is that the owner can't let something go to gain something. As time goes on, the sacrifice of profits for a short while might need to be made for growth to occur. This is true when we begin to hire people to replace us. It is also true of investing money to scale up a business, such as advertising. The goal of my advice for you is to help you find a way to reduce your workload as the owner so you can focus on growth and opportunity in the future.

Toss The Hats

When a person opens up their own business, they often try to wear all hats at once. They don't have the funds to hire an office manager, a receptionist, a financial advisor, or legal counsel. However, doing these tasks keeps you, the owner, from building the business. It's essential to learn different roles so you can duplicate them in the office, but mistakes and redundant strategies persist, and most importantly, loss of potential revenue. Keep in mind that as your business grows through the great marketing strategies you learn in this book, that you cannot allow yourself to get stuck doing everything alone. Remember why you started your business in the first place; wearing too many hats is not financial freedom, my friend. By five years in the business, you should have all the kinks worked out and trusting the processes you formulated are running smoothly. You then can take an extended vacation whenever you want and feel confident that your business will not fall apart while away.

Always be on the lookout for quality help. And at the first opportunity, make sure you have these tasks handled by professionals in their field. Hiring out tasks can feel intimidating to the beginner entrepreneur. You must decide if you can afford it, do your research to find the best candidate for the task, whether to hire a subcontractor or employee and if you have time to train an employee. Take your time with this one. One cautious step at a time is my advice. Before long, your well-oiled machine will produce a well-spring of cash flow without much effort. It's hard work getting to this point, but it's worth its weight in gold:

- Labor Work
- SalesForce
- Accounting and Financial Planning
- Taxes
- Office Management
- Legal Advising and Counseling
- Call Services
- Marketing & Advertising

THE LIST above are the hats, and you are the head it rests upon until you decide when to take it off and delegate the responsibility of the hat to someone else. If you don't have the professional skill to do the work, don't. Specialize your focus to building your business and satisfying your customers.

Leadership

If you go to your local bookstore, one of the most extensive sections and highly written about subjects is leadership. Governing the acts of other people has been analyzed, ridiculed, structured, and restructured since the dawn of time. And to this day, there are still hundreds of 'experts' who say theirs is the only way of managing a workforce.

TRUTH BE TOLD, the only thing you really need to know is respect begets respect. If you want others to follow your lead, you have to show them you can lead. Give them a reason to follow you that will be advantageous for them. If you don't have your 'team' on board with your ideas and goals, you'll be doing most of the heavy lifting without trust or respect for others. A good rule of thumb is always to be willing to do yourself what you ask others to do for you. Don't be that guy who tells your team to do something you snub your nose at doing. I have been in the presence of greatness in leadership, and I have witnessed losers whom I cannot figure out how they got into their positions as managers or supervisors.

MY FATHER WAS a business owner for 45 years. I would go to his office on the weekends to clean for some extra money in my youth. He cleverly asked me (after I committed to the job, of course) to report back to him if any of his employees complained about him to other employees. I never ratted on his employees. Years later, when he asked me to take over his business, I declined because of his "x-theory" methods of running a company with 15 employees. He always claimed that his employees were stealing from him, and no one was ever loyal.

I KNEW THE REASON WHY; my father verbally abused his employees. I knew early in the game that you can't get anyone to follow you if they have no respect for you. Respect is earned not by threats and coercion but by mutual respect and sensitivity toward them. Go back to the "Golden Rule" again, and live it. You can never go wrong. Mutual respect does not mean you should be a "friend" to your employees or "dip your pen in company ink," as they say. A leader is decisive, has a direction and is slow to speak because he listens to others.

Plan and Execute

A sure way of getting respect from your employees and sharing your goals is to visualize ahead of time with confidence, be decisive and give credit where and when credit is due.

BE PREPARED: If you are conducting a meeting, writing an email, making a phone call, or compiling data for a report, visualize beforehand what you want the result to be. Always govern your actions by the same rules you've trained your personnel. 'Do As I Do' is a powerful example and shows your employees you aren't afraid to get shoulder to shoulder with them if the situation arises.

THINK ON YOUR FEET: I'm speaking of the times when prudence, judgment, and circumstances determine the best possible solution for an opportunity or situation. When you suddenly face a decision, make sure you have all the facts and consider outcomes. Over time, the experience you gain will ease the pressure of your actions, but even so, you should be thinking "outside the box," looking into all possibilities creatively throughout your days, weeks, and years in your business. Don't discuss fleeting moments of thought with your team until you have considered all angles. It can be confusing for them and break down their feelings of security and well-being. Wait until you have thought things through before discussions with your team.

. . .

Give credit where credit is due: One of the best leadership traits is to give credit to whoever deserves the attention. When you recognize someone else for their skill or decision-making, you show them you noticed their actions and appreciate them for a well-done job. The admiration and dedication you'll receive after doing this, even one time, will prove to instill ambition and loyalty from your associates immediately. A recommended book on the subject of leadership, "The 21 Irrefutable Laws of Leadership: *Follow Them and People Will Follow You*" by John Maxwell

Summary

Be willing to make some sacrifices to allow growth by hiring others to lighten your workload.

Learn the core values of leadership so your team will desire to be loyal to you and your company. Professionalism enhances leadership abilities in planning and executing projects, meetings, and objectives.

Your team needs to feel secure in their job for reasonable productivity. Keep fleeting thoughts and ideas in a journal rather than tell your team until an appropriate time.

In the next chapter, you will learn to accomplish and follow through with negotiating contracts and avoiding pitfalls commonly experienced in the business world.

8
CONTRACTS

"Have the dogged determination to follow through to achieve your goal; regardless of circumstances or whatever other people say, think, or do." ~ Paul Meyer

In this chapter, I'll go over the details of client relations, negotiating contracts, and making sure you and your clients are entering into a fair, mutually respected business agreement.

NOT TOO LONG AGO IN history, it was expected that a deal would be made on a handshake and a promise for delivery. I personally don't know how anything ever got done back then. Maybe it was common that merchants in business had integrity, or it was assumed that everyone would be good for his word. Today, if anyone approached me this way, I would know, at the very least, he is inexperienced in business, and I don't want to deal with him even if he might be trustworthy. I have learned over the years that everything must be stated in a contract because if something is left out, it can be used in a nefarious way by a clever thief. And that is truly why contracts are needed in business. Nowadays, clever thieves can come in the form of major corporations or small business owners, even the old lady who seemed so nice. (yes, that's right!). The protection of contracts leaves nothing to chance, and the longevity of your business depends on it. I am a firm believer in solid, iron-clad contracts.

If there's one thing I've learned about contracts, it's this: Many clients will never read their contract but will sign their name to it. Never put critical information in small print, especially if it's in the contract. Any information pertinent to you receiving payment, dates of installation, or any other essential details, state them openly and clearly in different places. Discuss them personally, state them in emails, and list them on invoices. Never assume they have read the contract or have been attentive to the facts stated in your contract. If there is any problem with the job, that's when a client may read a contract or take note of dates.

Likewise, for every contract you receive from clients, sewing manufacturers, welders, contractors, or subcontractors, make sure you read the contract thoroughly and have your legal counsel, and sometimes your accountant, look them over also. If there are any discrepancies or questions, bring them up as quickly as possible so that the client can make corrections, and transactions can resume in a timely fashion.

. . .

ON LARGE JOBS, our company would assemble a pre-construction package with all information in detailed descriptions before the project begins. Think of it as a detailed project guide for the client, professionally assembled with correct costs, specific times, and delivery dates. This package would state all materials used, right down to the screw types, installation methods, and timelines. All information and work to be done should be listed before the project begins. Having everything stated and agreed upon before beginning work can save time, money, and unnecessary discussions throughout the job. This well-documented description will inform everyone about the project and expectations to anticipate when the job is completed. The client's signature validates it, so your company is covered if any legal issues come up. Make sure everyone is on the same page for the project. You can create a template on your computer by accessing a form on the internet or creating your own.

I CALL this pre-construction package PITA Protection: A preventative measure to avoid "Pain In The Ass" conflicts later. It will also serve you well to have this kind of professional document in place, not for the obvious reasons I've stated. You want to avoid any opportunity that would result in you not getting paid from the client or extra expenses on the project due to lack of communication.

The Devil is in the Details

Depending on whom you are working with, either you or your client can begin the contract process. If your client draws up the contract, they will add your invoice into their contract. This is fine; just follow the suggestions below to make sure you both are content with the process of the tasks at hand.

No CONTRACT IS EVER SET in stone except your company's Terms and Conditions. These should be a constant throughout your business career, with well-maintained and updated information that your client and her team can understand without an attorney deciphering it. Have your legal counsel put together your terms and conditions, so all statements will be legal and honored by a court of law. If you cannot afford an attorney initially, you can access copyright-free templates online.

I HATE to paint a grim picture, but the devil is in the details with all contracts, so to speak. If anything is left obscure, ambiguous, or too general, terms can be misinterpreted and used against your company if something goes wrong. During your career as an entrepreneur dealing with clients, someone will try to take advantage of your benevolence if you don't cover all the bases. I want to think all humans are gracious and considerate, but if they feel they've been wronged (just as you and I would), or just plain evil, they want to take the upper hand and see that issues fall in their favor. If you state all conditions in the contract, it doesn't matter what they say or do. You've complied with the contract and have protected yourself and your business from harmful situations.

. . .

You may need to have your legal counsel approve your clients' Terms and Conditions as well. Do not skim over contracts from your clients! Make sure you read them thoroughly because, unfortunately, all small businesses live in a world where many employees are taught by their bosses how to choose a small company unaware of unethical corporate tactics that will cripple your company if you are unaware. Never trust anyone! Please keep it simple, but again, have your legal counsel compile and approve all contracts and paperwork if something is unclear to you.

As I said before, in case you missed it, do not negotiate your Terms and Conditions contract if you have a potential client who wants to alter any wording or conditions. Kindly explain your terms to the client before they sign if they don't understand. If they are uncomfortable with your fair terms, back out of the proposition and find a client who respects your position. (Yes, we know that it is hard to back out of a $50k deal, but other better deals will come in due time) remember that your terms and conditions, if compromised, could land you in the poorhouse with no way out. We have found that our contracts are fair and reasonable for our clients, and if they have an issue, it's because our contract is too tight for them to squeeze out unethical practices against our company.

In only a few cases, a client will try to haggle on our 50% deposit requirement or the 10-day final payment after completion of the project. I could tell you some stories about how some companies have tried to get something for nothing, and some friends who lost their businesses due to lack of experience in getting worked over by the client. (The reason I wrote this book) Too many stories to tell for the scope of this book. Don't let my warnings scare you out of owning your own company, though, because bosses of corporations can treat their employees just as bad or worse. You have to watch for the red flags by following the instructions in these chapters, gaining experience through trial and error, and yes, intuition, my friend. You have the right to kindly refuse service to anyone you choose not to work with. Trust me when I say this: If you follow my instructions in this book, you will be able to spot the wolf long before he considers you for his dinner.

MAKE sure you have conditions in place for non-compliance to your terms. (what will happen to the client if they break the contract) For example, some damage has been done on the property after the contract is signed, and the installers get blamed for it. Yes, this situation does happen. Not so much anymore because video cameras are everywhere, but what then? Conditions will need to be stated on the outcome of such circumstances. As you move through your business experience, you will most likely update these conditions to include additional terms when you realize any issues that come up. Include them all! If you can't afford legal council just yet, terms and conditions contracts can be found on any website by searching the bottom of any site in small print. You can tailor anything to your company's needs as a guideline but never copy them verbatim. Plagiarism is easy to spot on the internet with algorithms in place just for that. Also, some copyright-free templates might be available to download for free; then you can tailor them to fit your company's needs. Keep in mind that evildoers hate tight contracts and will stay away.

When you or your team goes to a property for inspections and measurements, here is an opportunity to meet the client if possible, and possibly a few employees may engage in short conversation if you are at shopping centers. Employees can be valuable to understanding if problems exist with the current awning on the walls. Take their comments or complaints into consideration while you evaluate.

Thorough Inspections

You also have to be extremely thorough in your inspections. If you are mounting your structure to a compromised wall or frame, you can be sure at some point (probably while still under warranty) that your fine work will fall victim to the poor structure it's mounted on. Make sure, if there is a problem with the attachment of the awning to the wall, consult the client immediately and come to a workable conclusion. Most of the time, in this case especially, we might be able to wrap the fabric over the existing frame without removing it from the wall, leaving the wall still intact and uncompromised. Include your inspection findings in the pre-construction package mentioned in this book. If you come to an impasse on the security of the walls, back out of the deal and consider yourself lucky. No matter the quality of your work, if the wall is not sound, your awning can loosen with one high wind day and fall on an unsuspecting patron.

. . .

NOTE: When you are awarded a job before the contract is signed and negotiations are still being discussed, ensure all factors and details concerning your side of the job are clearly stated in a pre-construction package.

DURING INSPECTIONS, make certain situations like the one mentioned previously are written into your contracts, and your customer is aware of your concerns. For example, you see water damage or weak foundations that your awning will connect to, discuss this with your client and state any future damage that may come to your installation and structure. We found, in this example, that our client kept avoiding the conversation (Big Red Flag). Perhaps within the warranty period of your installation, the stabilized attachments fail, and the awning suffers, a client may blame you for poor quality installation and construction. They may even go so far as to blame you for the water damage in the walls or the foundation's weakness or stress. We were experienced enough to recognize a problem, but we were desperate for the $50k shopping center project with 950 yards of fabric going into the order. We decided to take the job and state in the contracts that we were aware of the water damage to the storefronts and weak walls. (because the employees told us) Adding into the pre-construction package that awning frames would not be removed from the walls, but only screw in loose fittings if necessary. The client was not happy about the frames not being removed (I wonder why) but agreed to the terms and handed us a check for $25K for the deposit. We took the job and completed it within the timeframe of the contract and waited 2 or 3 months for the final check to come. It was supposed to arrive ten days after completion of the project, which obviously did not. We ended up contacting a collection agency to get the remaining $25k from the property management company. The entire project was just not worth the trouble, even though it was a big one. The red flags were evident to us initially, but we ignored them because the dollar signs motivated us. When red flags appear, enter at your own risk.

OUR INVOICES now include a clause saying, "Installation as a Courtesy to Customer," meaning we don't charge them to be on their property. Clever huh? We still charge them to install, but it's fit into the price of manufacturing. This one statement may ensure your company's protection from possible lawsuits. Make sure you are covering everything necessary to keep your business safe. Just make sure the client realizes the risk of using old, weak, or damaged structures for bracing. Remember to do your inspections thoroughly and be prepared to walk away from a job if it won't complement your work.

A WORD **here about techy stuff:** Never remove a frame from the wall to re-cover it unless it is not attached to the wall in the first place. Some frames are held up by "Z brackets," not the wall.

Who is the Client?

Most often, you will be working with a manager or representative of the owner of the business. Ensure the person signing is the one who will be making the decisions for work upgrades, corrections, and addendums to the contract. If you feel someone else needs to be notified of the procedures, send a copy to the owner, president, or governing supervisor. Cover yourself as much as possible, and don't leave yourself exposed for a higher authority to take over the reins and derail your goodwill or good work. Consult your legal counsel with any situations or details you feel may pose as problematic.

Your job is to provide excellent professional service and quality materials/installation consistently. You can solve any problem that exists without compromising your integrity. Please do not break your own rules for a self-important client who promises you more work in the future (which likely will never happen) or asks for extended work without paying for it. Clients will respect you and your company if you don't allow them to be pushy about a 50% deposit or net 30 or 60 on final payments as well. Remember, the devil is in the details.

Negotiate Until Satisfied

Bids are just that, a bid: An estimation of what a job will need before work is scheduled and contracted out. It is within your rights to discuss details and processes until you precisely have the working situation you prefer. You can always walk away from any bid. Keeping this in mind, but don't cause friction if there isn't a viable problem.

It is imperative to maintain your integrity as an awning supplier, manufacturer, or distributor. Although underbidding a job sometimes happens with inexperienced contractors, the client will never give your company a good review or hire you again for a project if you grossly underbid and ask for more money in the middle of a project unless they ask for more work or different products or services.

EARLY IN OUR BUSINESS, we underbid a job or two or because of unexpected circumstances that we could not avoid. Still, we never asked the clients for more money than initially agreed upon by both parties. Our objective in keeping to this quote was integrity and nothing else.

ALWAYS ASK for at least a 50% deposit for any job, but increase the deposit amount if they want a specialty material that is a notably upscale material brand. We then add a discount to lower the project's overall cost if our numbers overbid the competition. If the client can't come up with the deposit, wait on beginning production until they can. And, once again, don't compromise your position for theirs. They need a quality awning or shade structure, and you are the company providing this for a reasonable price.

NEVER COMPROMISE your business terms for someone else's lack. This type of client, and you will experience them, are not looking for a quality awning; they are looking for a 'deal,' one that will undercut your profit and integrity. Walk away from the job; you won't miss their money or the headaches these people bring. Or you can do like we did and not listen to your intuition and experience a strained relationship with your client long after the job is completed. It's a sad story of frustration we experienced because of our desperation in the Tampa area early in our business partnership.

Deadlines and Completion Dates

When bidding out a job, always consider a timeline and then add a margin for error to be safe. You can always over-deliver and complete a job earlier. If you delay a job past the contract date, the client has leverage over your contract terms, quality, and any possibility of a reorder or bad review.

RISE above the competition by being honest in your dealings in all ways, including deadlines. Never say you can deliver on a deadline if you have a hard time seeing how you can do it. If you don't, it can cost you in the long run and will taint your reputation. We found it common for some awning companies to promise turnarounds of up to two weeks, unheard of in our industry. Of course, if you run into delays along the way, advise the client immediately, but take just a few steps initially to foresee any delays that may occur. Make sure before you call the client about any problems, have a serious business meeting with yourself or your team. You'll save yourself grief and stress, but often by delivering 'early,' you may prove to be the hero!

Tips For Longevity

Some of these points may be obvious to you, but I'm mentioning all of them because everyone is on a different learning curve:

. . .

Never use low-quality supplies and materials: Doing so takes money out of your pocket (and food off your table!). There are always ways to skimp on quality, and if you do, you will need to re-visit the past client with their problem awning, or worse, they will leave you a bad review, and you lose business as a result.

Warranties are not negotiable: Decide on a warranty and stick to it throughout your business and design. Altering your warranty creates chaos in your business plan and confuses repeat customers. State the warranty and be done with it. After completing a project, we send the client an email with links to warranties and cleaning instructions. They receive a Q.R. code sticker for the "all" program placed on the window or tag at the awning's edge for visibility.

Summary

Stay the course and keep an eye on your goals without compromising your terms and conditions. Some clients are trained by their bosses to try to negotiate lower prices or change your terms, and you must not give in. Remember, you have the right to do business with whomever you want, and you are allowed to drop them as a client if no contracts are signed yet.

Contracts are your statement of each project: What you'll do, at what cost you'll do it, and under what circumstances you'll be doing them. Be thorough, be detailed, and be direct.

. . .

ON LARGE PROJECTS, formulate a pre-construction package for your client. This document should be signed by all parties (sometimes notarized) to ensure they understand the details of the project undertaken.

NEGOTIATIONS MEAN JUST THAT, negotiate, and do this until you are 100% satisfied.

NEVER SACRIFICE quality materials because the lower-priced supplies are truly low-quality products.

IN THE NEXT CHAPTER, you'll find all the intricacies and details of making your job enjoyable because you will be able to avoid problems in your business.

NOTES:

_____
_____
_____
_____
_____
_____
_____
_____
_____
_____

9

POLISHING YOUR PROCEDURES

"Success is; knowing what you're doing, loving what you're doing, and believing what you're doing."
  ~ *Napoleon Hill*

Now, it's time to start your engines!

As I've said many times, you only need a computer and printer, a phone, a mailing box, and an internet connection. These are apparent tools for every entrepreneur. However, I'd like to give you some suggestions which have made our lives easier through the years in the awning industry. Each of these suggestions had improved our company's efficiency and avoided setbacks before they became issues. I'm sure they will improve your business as well.

Action Steps

Often we can make the assumption that every business automatically knows how they are supposed to be "customer service oriented" and "professional". Still, I am continuously surprised by the lack of attention and understanding of the basic needs of customers by the companies that serve them. With the knowledge you have already gained in this book, you are significantly ahead of the competition in your chosen industry regarding these matters. There's no need to re-invent the wheel; it takes too long and slows down progress. Absorb information from those who came before you first; then your learning curve will accelerate.

I LEARNED that I needed to create my own tools for efficiency and money-saving tasks, which kept us several steps ahead of the competition and separated us from the crowd. In the list below are some suggestions I've developed as a result of frustrations I was experiencing in my day-to-day business dealings. Some will work for you, and others may not. But consider them wisely as you assemble your work ethic and business image.

- Keep a personal time journal and appointment book with you at all times. You may want to use your cell phone, which makes it very convenient to enter data, but it has happened a few times that my phone stopped working and I had no backup, so if you use this method, have a reliable data transfer service to upload on your computer automatically.

- Measure and inspect each project carefully and thoroughly before and during the job. If two awnings look the same, don't assume they are. Measure all of them to avoid a hairy situation from occurring in the future of the project. If you ignore this advice, I promise that somewhere down the line, overlooking this simple procedure will cost your company lots of $$$

- Take before and after photos of each job and send the client completed work images. You can proudly post before and after photos of your work on your site and social media, and awning shoppers will love it! Also, B2B clients may not ever go to the property they commissioned your work for, and they will need several photos of the finished work sent to them. Being diligent about doing this even before they ask for them will be a thoughtful gesture in your clients' eyes.

- Take a clipboard or notepad with you wherever you go with extra "call forms" so you can take new client calls and have a record of information. You will also send them an email right away during or after the call, if possible. Keep your potential clients interested.

- Keep fabric samples, business cards, and a measuring device in your vehicle at all times. You always want to be prepared for anything.

- Schedule 'excess' time in your day for unplanned tasks or meetings

- Consider implementing a "photo quoting program" on your website: Your potential client sends pictures for you to work up your bid form. By using photos, you can save travel time and give your potential client a quick turnaround quote. By doing this, you also increase the opportunity for them to move forward to a project agreement quickly, before getting other comparison bids or missing the initial excitement of your client.

- Never tell the potential client an estimate of a job on the phone or in a face-to-face meeting. Doing this diminishes the value of your business to the client in the awning industry. They may ask you over and over again, resist the temptation to do it by kindly declining to answer this question.

- After a job is complete, ask for a 5-star review from your satisfied clients. In the B2B sector, this can be pretty difficult because some companies do not allow their employees to give reviews, but small business owners are usually delighted to give one. It never hurts to ask!

Your Office

As with your business image, you will have preferences in your office equipment. Just because we use one particular type doesn't mean it is the catch-all for everyone. Make sure that your office is a creative space and not a cluttered place. Keep the light bright, and give yourself plenty of room to move around. Confinement and low-grade lighting can funk your mood and your mindset. If you aren't open for growth and constantly thinking forward, your business will follow you in the same manner, and both of you will stagnate. I like a comfortable couch in my office for taking a 15-minute mental break, but make sure you set the alarm to wake you up. I find it very refreshing only if it doesn't go past 15 minutes!

Here's a brief run-down of the individual office equipment we have found to be the best for our business and we use and why we use it.

Computers: Though I'm sure P.C.s are powerful and user-friendly, we've always used MacBook Pro laptop computers. Their graphics stand-alone in ease of use and design capabilities. We've always used the Apple brand, so to change at any point along the way seemed futile for us. The learning curve alone would have been an unnecessary stressor. I also like to take my office everywhere (hence, the laptop) and not be confined to my home office.

Handheld Devices: Once again, the iPhone is our choice. They sync beautifully with the computer, and we can interchange files, images, and photos easily. Because we are in the 'field,' having an assimilated system gives us streamlined benefits and few challenges. And now, the added iPad technology is almost as good as having a face-to-face meeting in a conference room. We can connect over the internet and have virtual conferences on design, changes, upgrades, communication, and deliveries. We can now do just about anything we would have done in a personal contact meeting through devices and the internet. It saves both our clients and our time and money, also, recent compliance to no-contact regulations.

IF YOU ARE able to afford the additional equipment, you can use an iPad or P.C. Tablet and download the Awning Composer software. Use it in the field if you prefer meeting face to face with the client for immediate viewing of an upgraded building/awning design for your client. Be sure to practice using the software beforehand.

GRAMMARLY: The Software is so easy to use and download; it's an intelligent way to have all-in-one spellcheck, word suggestion, and grammar correcting application when composing emails, contracts, letters, blogs, and website content. If anything makes you look uneducated, it's conveying poor grammar and multiple mistakes in your communications. Your reader will be distracted by your lousy grammar and disrespect for your image as well as your intellect. Basic Grammarly is free, and it works just fine for whatever communication media you are writing. Trust me; you'll have a professional appearance both in person and in all your communications.

FINANCIAL SOFTWARE: In addition to having your accountant who advises you and handles your financial statements and taxes, you'll also want a compatible software program to enter in the pricing and costs for invoicing clients, expenses, operations, and any other figures you use. Make sure your accountant works in the same program, so your files will transfer quickly across all transactions, and make sure the program is easy for you to use and update quickly. If you aren't comfortable with your software, you'll hate using it and end up entering all your data at the end of the month. If you like working in the software, you'll also keep up on the data input, and both you and your accountant will be happy with the process and outcome. We have always used Quickbooks as our financial software because it's very user-friendly. Others available are NetSuite and FreshBooks, but many are on the market. Please consult your accountant on the software they use. Try out a free trial or search for reviews on each.

Procedures for Bidding Jobs

Most often, I choose the most straightforward way I can do something which my business can afford. The Awning Composer is the only program I know of that formulates close to accurate quotes for any bid or project. It uses color 3D visuals to bring your projects to life, drops in measurements, and can do this from a downloaded photo. You can dress up your visuals or keep them simple. It can save you time and money while making your company look professional and well-prepared.

YOU CAN ALSO ADD customizable features, like frame style, fabric color and brand, valence styles, and various graphics choices. The new upgraded version allows you to create pricing from previously entered price lists and assemble an estimate package. All in all, I find Awning Composer easy to use, has clean and attractive visuals. It is inexpensive, and there is an option to try before you buy. Check it out to see if it works for you. Clients love to see a finished awning design for their wall but only use this feature if they are positively going with your company. Too often, they will try to wrap up all your time with different images they want to try. It is a time-consuming task, and as you know, time is money. Another option would be to charge them for different designs you create that you can discount from the project's cost. If you choose another subcontracting industry, there are many auto-cad specialty programs similar to this.

Working Up a Bid Manually

If you choose manual bidding and assemble your estimates without a program, follow the steps I've listed here. Keep in mind; you can raise or lower the figures I use, considering your experience, location, and supply costs. Assemble a price list from your suppliers and update it when costs change.

TOTAL ALL COSTS:

- Begin with the supply expenses, add labor costs, equipment needs, and other installation expenses.
- Calculate the total amount excluding your overhead for the month.
- Divide the monthly overhead cost by the number

of jobs projected for the month, then add that total into the previous amount.
- The total amount will be the 50% deposit.
- Multiply the total times 2 or 3 depending on the size of the project.

HERE'S a rule of thumb to remember: The smaller the job, the higher the cost per square inch or square foot of the awning. Sometimes your bid may be a bit high because specialty fabrics can get pretty pricey. After calculating supplies into the project: Here's where you can offer the client a discount if they pay 75% as a deposit.

SINCE YOU ARE JUST QUOTING the job without being hired for the project yet, you won't know the exact cost of everything, but you want to be as close as possible. At the end of the quote, add a small percentage of cushion for incidentals (mistakes in costs, cost increases between bid and contract signing, any miscalculations, miscellaneous). Always add an expiration date of 30 to 60 days to your quotes. Many B2B clients go beyond this time limit before finally beginning the project because they need to fit the cost into their quarterly budget (unless its an insurance claim)

STAY at your quote amount as a firm figure if at all possible. Our company takes pride in telling the customer that our quotes derived just from our photo quoting will not change, and it is the exact amount needed for the job. Experience and research will get your company to this point in the future. However, anything goes after the quote expires.

AND THERE YOU HAVE IT, the estimated price for a job. Each area in the U.S. has its price structure, so you get a clear idea of what you need when pricing jobs wherever you are. Also, make sure you are within range with your competitors. How do you know your quote is competitive with other companies if you are experienced in the industry? Homewyse.com is a great tool to confirm your awning pricing according to your area of business. In many industries, the same concept applies.

A Word on Merchant Accounts

In our continuous effort to be a progressive company, we tried using a merchant account for customer convenience as we were increasingly aware of their needs. However, in the awning business, this step proved to be in the wrong direction, and I am here to tell you why this is true. First of all, when we provide a quote for our clients, we offer the fairest price to them. If we used a merchant account, then we would have to tack on a percentage to the quote. 2.5% is extremely high if the deposit is $10k. Get my point? It's not worth the trouble for another reason also; if a client is unsatisfied with the work you provided or even pretends to be, it can spell disaster for your company. Regardless of your company is at fault or not, the merchant has the right to "remove" the funds from your business account until further notice of a resolution. You have to prove your innocence in this case. I am absolutely not a proponent of any company that has the authority to do so. (okay, I confess I didn't read the fine print)

We were caught up in this situation only once, and then I never used the services of a merchant account ever again. I realize some businesses cannot function too well without it, but if it doesn't make you more money to offset the risk, then it's not worth the trouble. The problems associated with the decision to use them caused us to rethink our choice of risking our necks to provide this service for our clients. I say no way!

Summary

As you assemble your business equipment and software, choose products that integrate easily with each other and are user-friendly.

Please review our list to heighten the quality of your business and streamline your process.

Keep your home office a space you enjoy, and set your alarm for frequent breaks to clear your mind. I use this time for a walk with my dog or a power nap.

Implement low-cost or free software for streamlining your process in financial, design, and quotes.

FINAL WORDS

∼

"Success consists of going from failure to failure without loss of enthusiasm." ~ Winston Churchill

And there you have it, all the do's and don't of running a successful and abundantly profitable awning business. I've given you the reasons why opening an awning and shade company or other outsourcing industry can bring you huge profits almost immediately. I've told you the essential things to set in place and the ones which may seem important but won't bring you money.

I've explained why each support needs to be in place, your support teams as well as equipment, and I've also explained why using them correctly and with professionalism will show your clients why you are their best choice.

You now have the tools to put the wheels in motion, and it's up to you to begin. If you are feeling a bit overwhelmed right now, follow these tips:

Start with the right attitude: You have to believe in yourself in order for others to believe in you. The world will try to beat you down, especially if you're not equipped with a support network of people who believe in your mission. Every day, no matter how you feel at any given moment, must be a positive magnet that attracts positive outcomes. What a man sows he shall reap, and what a man thinks he will become. It is critical to your success to capture every thought and make it positive. Your body will thank you too because, as the new quantum science suggests, your mind controls your body. Resistance to 'fear of the unknown' can be a futile task of the mind if the environment around it is agreeable to its terms. No one has the truth of you in a crystal ball, so you are the only catalyst for change. The force is already within you to become successful. Whatever personal or professional weaknesses you feel might hold you back from your future success, attack them with a vengeance to eradicate it. Whatever book you need to read, therapy, or family resolutions, do it. Take your time; you aren't in a race to the finish line. Follow the steps carefully!

Be thorough: No one ever won a race by being incomplete. Think the process through, check your work, and make sure you have others to help double-check your work. It's better to pay someone to support you than lose a client because you failed.

Choose your teams wisely: If you were thorough in just one area, let it be this one. Having a great team gives you peace of mind as well as more time to build your business. You will grow in confidence when you have a team of professionals who can confidently do what you ask of them and be there when you need them. When asked about how he achieved success, a wealthy businessman once said, "I am not smart; I just know how to get a great team who is."

Ask questions: Never feel like you are alone in your entrepreneurship. There are hundreds, if not thousands, who have started their new business in the last year. Reach out to associations and your community to gain knowledge and support and to develop contacts.

Know your region: Having a firm grasp of your community's needs and growth is a must. When you know how your local economy is growing, you will practically have an automatic client list. Be diligent in your research, and it will give you the answers and point you in the direction of growth every time.

There are several streams of income opportunities you can add to your company as you grow. Or maybe, you might like to focus on one of these for your initial business. For whatever reason, consider these additional ways to make money in the awning and shade structure industry:

- Create a D.I.Y. (do it yourself) awning product for basic measurements with easy install. Or purchase the "Smart Awning System" license to sell.
- Develop a lead generation and sale program for other awning and sign companies
- Focus on sub-contract networking and

membership site, connecting contractors you know with manufacturers in the industry.
- Start a franchise business to teach other entrepreneurs how to begin their awning and shade structure business. (must follow stringent guidelines for execution)
- Sell supplies for the industry, such as fabric, hardware, notions, and fabrication.
- Focus on a strictly commercial business, catering to more extensive jobs
- Focus on residential business, specializing in residential preferences and installations
- Begin a cleaning business for awnings, using the needed techniques to keep awnings structurally sound while making them look their best.

For those of you who are interested in the awning and shade industry, you will be highly rewarded for your choice of industries. Awning and shade structures have always been around in every culture on the planet, and they always will be around as long as the sun shines, and the clouds precipitate. Right now, you are on the verge of finding a pot of gold at the end of the rainbow!

For the rest of you who reached this point, you are not far behind with the knowledge I have shared with you. However, if you go off on your own without some guidance and direction away from what I have shared here, the road will be rocky. Don't go it alone. Whatever business venture you decide is right for you overall, remember this:

Nothing comes easy like a breeze on a cool day. Nope, it requires knowledge and research, unwavering commitment and consistency, and most of all, desire! Please make use of the resources provided and you will be on your way to freedom.

I hope this book has been just as enjoyable for you to read as it was for me writing it. If you absolutely appreciate this book and want to help out my cause to teach new entrepreneurs, "The Secret Online Business: *How to Start & Operate An Outsourcing Company from Home,*" will have it's best chance of distribution with your honest and detailed review by scrolling to the bottom of the book page on Amazon. Your review will be greatly appreciated!

If you have any questions or would like to provide constructive feedback with us please email the publisher directly at: info@drumrollpress.com and they will respond immediately. Thank you for your patronage!

REFERENCES AND SUGGESTED READING

Clear, J. (2019). Atomic Habits: *An Easy & Proven Way to Build Good Habits & Break Bad Ones*. Penguin Audio, an imprint of the Penguin Random House Audio Publishing Group.

Purvin, D. (2021). Business Owners MBA. https://www.businessownersmba.com/.

Robbins, A. (1997). Unlimited Power: *The New Science of Personal Achievement*. Simon & Schuster.

Abrams, R. (2019). Successful Business Plan Secrets & Strategies. Palo Alto, CA: PlanningShop.

Steingold, D. M., Atty. (2016). Nolo's Guide to Single-Member LLCs: *How to Form & Run Your Single-Member Limited Liability Company* (2nd ed.). Berkley, CA: Nolo.

Tyson, E., MBA, & Schell, J. (2020). Back to Basics: *Starting a Small Business* (B&N Exclusive Edition). Wiley.

Green, L. C., & Brown, P. B. (2017). The Entrepreneur's Playbook: *More than 100 Proven Strategies, Tips, & Techniques to Build a Radically Successful Business.* New York: Amacom.

Maxwell, J. C., & Covey, S. R. (2007). The 21 Irrefutable Laws of Leadership: *Follow Them and People Will Follow You* (10th anniversary ed.). HarperCollins Leadership.

www.ingramcontent.com/pod-product-compliance
Lightning Source LLC
Chambersburg PA
CBHW071504220526
45472CB00003B/909